TRUE BRIT

CLIVE IRVING

TRUE BRIT

JONATHAN CAPE
THIRTY BEDFORD SQUARE LONDON

FIRST PUBLISHED 1974
© 1974 BY CLIVE IRVING
JONATHAN CAPE LTD, 30 BEDFORD SQUARE, LONDON WCI

ISBN 0 224 01005 0

To William Cobbett, who saw it all coming

PRINTED IN GREAT BRITAIN BY
W & J MACKAY LIMITED, CHATHAM

Contents

Prologue

Even Sir Henry 'Chips' Channon, whose diaries are unmatched in revealing the insensibility of the true snob, was impressed: 'I have seen much, travelled far and am accustomed to splendour, but there has never been anything like tonight.' The entry was for July 7th, 1939. The event was the ball at Blenheim, that palace built by Marlborough on the proceeds of military genius and British chauvinism. The scene that met Chips's eyes was equal to the legend. The palace, the terraces and the lakes were floodlit; Tyrolean singers strolled among the seven hundred guests and the supply of champagne was unlimited. As Chips noted: 'It was all of the England that is supposed to be dead but isn't.'

'Après moi ...' Spectacular spasms of escapism tend to occur on the edge of apocalypse; at the time of the Blenheim ball, war was less than two months away.

In November 1973 a princess married a Dragoon and for twenty-four hours reality took a minor place in British news coverage. The timing was precarious. The day before, on November 13th, a set of disastrous trade figures precipitated panic on the London Stock Exchange. This was the first warning of a confluence of pressures which, within weeks, brought the nation to a peacetime crisis worse than most people had known in their lifetime.

But it took a long time to sink in; the carnival was reluctant to admit the crisis. At the Oxford and Cambridge rugby game in December the normal quota of Rolls-Royces turned up, and the usual quantities of champagne were guzzled, during what are known as normal office hours. The delay in facing facts was not really so surprising, since Edward Heath's government was steadfastly refusing to admit how bad things were. It clung to a congenitally Panglossian view.

This response was in character not only with that government but with much of the country. Diagnoses of the crisis usually centre on its economic and technical components. Some are valid, if unwelcome. But much of the real cause of the recurrent British tragedy is not technical, but emotional. Over a wide range of its affairs the country is self-deceiving.

This book is primarily about that emotional factor, and about a state of mind which made some kind of denouement inevitable. It might have come later, rather than sooner. It might have taken any one of a number of forms. The last resort of any government at a time of national collapse is to call for unity: ' ... in the end, our ability to survive, to beat inflation, depends on our willingness as a nation to act together and to act responsibly' – this was Edward Heath's appeal. But in Britain the real foundation for national unity, a shared sense of community, was missing.

To assume that the right climate did exist for that kind of appeal is only one of the many illusions which have proved remarkably resilient. Not only political policies, but some of our fundamental institutions rest on a similar capacity to defer reality. But first, before assessing these structural flaws, a substantial mythology has to be dismantled, and it is one which the British are not alone in clinging to.

Part One

Is anybody here in charge?

1 The Doctrines of True Brit: Sail on, all who still believe . . .

Britain is more than a country: it's an idea. For years now long after British power evaporated, the British idea has continued to fascinate people of all nationalities and races. Even those who were once under British rule, and are of normally sound mind, are drawn to the spell of the British idea.

The idea can be all things to all men. To a democrat it represents a system that works. To a conservative it shows the value of enduring standards. To a liberal it demonstrates the ideal of social tolerance. To a revolutionary like Marx it could offer both sanctuary and the frustrating triumph of gradualism. To the scholar it possesses the springs of eternal wisdom. To the Christian it is a place for solemn pilgrimage. To the sensualist it has acquired a new promise of pleasure. To the Latin it has an enviable reserve. To the pacifist it has humanitarian restraint. To the militarist it carries numerous honours in the arts of war. To the stylist it has style.

Make of it what they will, all Anglophiles share one belief in their allegiance to the British idea: it is the last civilization. Decline can be overlooked as long as virtue remains. If virtue were lost, the Anglophile's most valuable bearing would be gone: the British comparison. Every problem needs its antonym.

But many paragons are fraudulent. The British idea was always a muddle of inconsistencies, as much mystique as reality. It seems to me that now what reality once existed has gone. Many will find this hard to take. If sheer belief could have kept the British idea aloft it would have been willed immortality, a testament to the power of prayer. But, as in all affairs left to men, it was mortal.

Hard facts for the true believer

1. The British system works.

Nobody is sure what this system is. There is supposed to be something called 'Parliamentary government' in the care of the 'mother of Parliaments'. If that is so, the old girl is senile. While members of Parliament play elaborate procedural games and taunt each other with words, the power of Parliament has been steadily subverted by a non-elected bureaucracy. Simultaneously, the concept of rule by Cabinet has given way to a form of Presidential rule, in which the Prime Minister has recruited his own staff, with a heavy elitist bias, and through which policy decisions are virtually pre-ordained before they reach the Cabinet. This is a version of rule by 'expert'. Prime Ministers also cultivate their own coterie of like-minded spirits to evolve their singular philosophy for how the people shall live.

In effect, in recent years power in the country has passed into invisible hands. Any idea that the destiny of the people can be entrusted to Parliament is an offence to the expertise of the 'experts', who know that they know best.

Isn't this unconstitutional? It would be, if there were a Constitution. But the British are proud that their Constitution is unwritten, which means that you can make it up as you go along. A great deal of making up has been going on lately, probably more than at any time in British history, and certainly more than most of the British realize.

2. The British have a genius for changing without seeming to change.

This is true. For example, there has been a great redistribution of wealth in Britain. Instead of allowing all the country's wealth to remain in the hands of landed aristocrats, industrial plutocrats, and financiers, some of it has been redirected into the hands of property speculators, asset-strippers, and new financiers.

3. The Welfare State takes good care of the poor.
The Welfare State was a good idea, but it was overtaken by the Corporate State. The idea of the Corporate State is to make everybody richer by taking money from taxes and passing it to all the businessmen who know how best to use it for the national interest. In the meantime, several million people in Britain are living at, or below, the poverty line. Two-and-a-half million are living in houses which are for-givingly described in officialese as 'unfit' – which means that they lack amenities like hot water, a bath, or an indoor lavatory. What they don't lack is squalor. When the British businessmen have made things come right there might be money left over to take care of such minor inconveniences.

4. The British have their priorities right.
That depends on who you are. If you are in urgent need of an aeroplane to fly the Atlantic in three hours at something more than the regular first-class fare, then they have the plane for you. On the other hand, you may think it un-reasonable to spend £760m. of public funds to provide such a convenience when, for the same money, you could get two new cities or several hundred hospitals and schools.

5. Class is no longer important in Britain.
There are basically two kinds of school in Britain: state schools and independent schools. The state schools are free, the independent schools require many parents to pay fees of as much as £1,000 a year. In 1971, 31·5 per cent of the boys going to independent schools went on to university; 5·7 per cent of the boys going to state schools qualified for and entered university. The number of children going to independent schools actually went down by 2 per cent between 1961 and 1971, but they remain the best bet for parents who want to get their children into Oxford or Cam-bridge. And an Oxbridge education remains the magic key to both a high-status career and the subtle social network that in Britain still fixes things in its own quiet way.

6. British justice is the fairest in the world.
Neither British judges nor British courts may be held in
contempt. Contempt of court is a serious offence. This
makes commentary on the courts difficult. For example, if
you happened to be the parent of a child mutilated before
birth by a drug called thalidomide, and you had spent years
waiting to get compensation out of the company which
made the drug, and a newspaper took up your case and
sought to make that company feel shameful in public –
where would the public interest lie? In the view of the Law,
the newspaper is making a mischief. Distillers, the company
which made the drug, ought not – said the court – to be
'pressured' on behalf of limbless children. Such pressure,
while the company and parents deliberated, is 'contempt of
court'. The newspaper should hold its peace. The children
should carry on waiting for the lawyers to agree.

7. The British policeman is the finest in the world.
In 1972, among the elite of the British police at Scotland
Yard, 144 officers were admitted to have been 'in serious
trouble'. Eighty of them had 'retired early'. Some were
trafficking in drugs, some were taking bribes, some were
keeping strange company.

8. The British civil servant is the most honest in the world.
Right. But you might be forgiven for the wicked thought,
after studying his record, that corruption could be more
efficient and less costly than integrity. Once it passes into
the hands of the British civil service, money seems to de-
crease markedly in value and effectiveness.

9. There are no serious racial problems in Britain.
Between 1948 and 1972 about one million West Indians,
Asians and Africans came to live in Britain, their 'mother'
country; another half-million blacks were born British. At
first they were called 'settlers'; then 'coloured'; then 'immigrants'; then it was suggested that they might like to go
back where they came from – even those who had been born
in Britain. In 1964 a Tory campaigned on the ticket 'If you

want a nigger neighbour, vote Labour'. In 1968 the Rt. Hon. Enoch Powell, M.P., said that allowing in the blacks was 'like a nation busily engaged in heaping up its own funeral pyre'. As the man who had dared to say in public what had only been whispered in private, Powell became the overnight idol of white supremacists. While they condemned Powell, both Labour and Tory governments tightened the screw on immigration until by the early 1970s it had virtually dried up.

By then, the blacks had taken their place in British society. At the bottom. Their company was not wanted, but their utility was undeniable. They do the jobs that whites find distasteful.

10. British inventiveness has inspired the world.
True: they invented paper money and the Industrial Revolution – but only at the cost of industrial pollution, child labour, and sweated labour. Being great respecters of tradition, the British revere the old values wherever possible.

11. Suddenly the British are sexy.
Not suddenly; they've just been enjoying it more – or more of them have been caught enjoying it, particularly the upper classes. The upper classes always did enjoy it, but they used not to be caught. Sex was once thought too good for the lower classes, so the upper classes imagined they had kept the secret to themselves. Sex was not, after all, as the prosecutor of *Lady Chatterley's Lover* had inferred, something you would want your servants to read about. However, the word has got out. Given the knowledge and given the pill, the working class are enjoying it so much that they have had to be tartly reminded that they didn't invent it. All this has been very provocative for the Puritans, who tried to stamp it out. And just to prove that it was democratic, a government minister who was also a Lord was caught with his pants down, *à trois*, with the help of a two-way mirror. In London, the two-way mirror business is booming.

12. There is no corruption in British public life.

Corruption runs through all levels of British public life: it is pervasive but not normally conspicuous. There is a long-established and carefully refined way of acting corruptly. A great deal of corruption in Britain is petty. Twenty pounds will easily buy a man. Careers have been finished by the temptations of a few bottles of whisky, a holiday in Majorca, a swimming pool in the yard. There's a subtle, interlocking brotherhood with connexions in every town – and there's always the right man to see. Two things enable this system to flourish: its enormous discretion, and the absence of any tradition of muckraking. When the muck does get raked, very rarely, and usually by accident, there is a general howl in the land. In such bouts of self-righteousness a handful of fall-guys are pilloried, usually the small fry, and many fine words spoken about the exception proving the rule.

13. Made in Britain means made by craftsmen, with love.
There is more craftiness than craft. Nobody has turned anachronism to advantage like the British. Look at our castles, they say, and then they add: our cars are built like that. But, with some rare exceptions, that car comes off a production line just like any other, except that the factory is probably older than most. A sleek line and a good painting job can still conceal a lot of trouble, and often do. In a world where almost anything falls to bits, the British want you to believe that their stuff won't. Why should they be so lucky?

14. The British are kind to animals, children, and anyone in need; their word is their bond; they honour God and follow His commandments; they ...
But enough. If the True Believer has come thus far, he will want evidence. These are serious charges; idols cannot lightly be tarnished.

The last people to give up the British idea will be the British themselves. There is a certain justice in this. The less real the idea gets to everybody else, the more the British hang on to it. It is a collective hallucination, remarkably durable. This state of mind shall be known as True Brit.

The essence of True Brit is a belief in one's country's greatness. More than that, it is to believe that this greatness is God-given. Other countries are not immune to the greatness bug, though it expresses itself differently. In America it's a question of quantity; in France a question of style; in Russia a question of sheer weight. To the British it's a question of quality. True Brit is taken in with the mother's milk. And if it isn't, a British education will rectify the error.

Until not so long ago the teaching of history in British schools centred on the parts marked red on the globe: the stain of empire on which the sun never set. With that gone, there is plenty of greatness left. British history as presented in school is still a perpetual rerun of fables, lies, and prudent editing. Defeats are allowed as a fleeting counterpoint before the next trumpet blast. Sometimes defeat is transmuted into victory, like that of Dunkirk.

The greatness of True Brit has two threads: military power and economic power. Both are sanitized as things used in saintly missions. In this respect, True Brit does less than justice to the British. The emphasis on martial clout makes muscle more important than mind. Here's a typical evocation of True Brit, written by Tom Stacey in *The Times* as Britain joined the European Common Market:

> We are still capable of speaking about 'us' and 'our nation' and know what we mean. There is succour there from our inherited characteristics, our shared heroes, our victories and even our defeats. Drake, Wellington, Churchill. The defeat of the Armada. Waterloo, Dunkirk. Shakespeare, Dickens, Hardy. Our sense of fair play, and a very high grade of humour, law, government, horti-culture and breakfast.

Horticulture and breakfast?

But note that Wellington comes before Shakespeare, and that Newton gets no mention at all. The really civilizing British ideas were secondary to the Bible-thumping that went with colonial aggression. It was not the British culture that 'civilized' the primitives, but the British boot and the British gun. True Brit appeals to the philistine, not the aesthete.

True Brit fosters three kinds of myth: institutional, personal, and symbolic. The institutional myths enable the British to feel that they enjoy an immunity to social instability – British law, Parliament, and even the police are inviolate. The personal myths are, but for that of the monarchy, all in the past. The most recent is the myth of Churchill, still a deity. A personal myth may extend to some of the symbolic myths. John Bull, so readily evoked by Churchill, began his career as a curious blend of squire and rustic, a symbol of pugnacity and probity. Later he became a chauvinist. Sometimes symbolic myths become quasi-institutional, like that of Rolls Royce, which transcends prosaic engineering and, to the patriot, is shorthand for excellence. The Bank of England is not just the national treasury but a symbol of native integrity and solvency. All these myths, so embedded in True Brit, seemed as secure as they were indispensable. But they have turned out to be false.

True Brit assumes an ethnic certainty, a belief that there is an Anglo–Saxon racial purity dating from the moment when that extra share of greatness arrived as divine gift. In truth, British blood is polygenetic.

The English millennium was supposed to be complete in 1973. In 973, King Edgar, great-grandson of Alfred, was crowned at Bath, becoming by legend the first King of England. But it depended on what was meant by England. There was another claimant, Egbert, crowned King of England in 829, which – if the claim was valid – made the millennium more than 130 years late. Elizabeth II, that matronly monarch of German lineage, was happy to endorse Edgar, perhaps because it seemed a good time to boost True Brit with a piece of pageant. But Edgar was something of a mongrel.

His line had fused Angles, Saxons, and the ancient

Hebrews ('Zadok the Priest' was sung at his Coronation). Since then the English crown has been claimed by a variety of tribes.

But the consuming belief in True Brit overlooks such details. Nothing seems able to deter it. In a prolonged and petty fight with the Icelanders over fishing rights, the British trawler skippers were gripped by some fantasy of everlasting naval supremacy. They asked for support from the Royal Navy, and when they got it they played 'Rule Britannia' over ship-to-shore radio.

True Brit sails on, wearing an imbecilic smile.

2 *The Paupers of Europe*

The British woke up one morning and found themselves the paupers of Europe. The most galling thing about this was the prosperity of the French and the Germans. The average British view of a Frenchman is either of a garlic-chewing peasant labouring in feudal backwaters, or a perfumed adulterer indulging his *cinq à sept*. About the Germans he feels even less warm.

In 1958 the French gross national product was 25 per cent below the British; it is now (in 1973) more than 25 per cent ahead of it. Measured by personal income, the most prosperous part of Britain, the south-east, is equal to the poorest part of France, the south-west. Parisians are markedly richer than Londoners. Most of Britain is poorer than anywhere in Europe except middle and southern Italy, and a part of Belgium. Germany is the richest of all, overtaking even the U.S.A. for the first time in 1973. In world rank Britain is sixth, exactly half as wealthy as Germany.

What is worse, Dr Hermann Kahn's crystal ball predicts that by 1985 Britain will be in ninth or tenth place in Europe, lagging behind Spain, Austria, and Greece. The richest will be France, outstripped in the world only by the U.S.A. and Japan. Admittedly, this humiliating prognosis was commissioned from Dr Kahn by the French government, conveniently just before an election. Asked for a less statistical and more psychological explanation for British collapse, Kahn says:

> In Britain more than anywhere else there is respect for old wealth but hostility to new wealth. The difference is

that with new wealth and rapid growth the rich get richer and the poor get richer too. With slow growth like yours the rich get richer and the poor get poorer.

In fact, social wealth and corporate wealth in Britain are in stark contrast. British companies are by far the most profitable in Europe: in 1971 sixty-three of the top 100 European companies judged by profit were British, only thirteen were German, and seven French. Kahn's thesis of polarized rather than evenly distributed wealth is valid. Britain has the most innately unbalanced society in Europe.

There is no mystery about where those company profits go: to the richest minority. Ninety-five per cent of privately controlled shares in Britain are owned by 5 per cent of the population, and this top 5 per cent own nearly half of the personal wealth of the country. The inequality of wealth in Britain is now about the same as in the U.S.A.: in both countries the top one per cent own about a quarter of the total wealth on latest estimates.

Just how rich the richest are is hard to tell, because wealth in Britain is not brandished. It reposes discreetly away from vulgar view in large estates sculptured by generations of landscape gardeners. By far the most consistent movement of wealth is not from rich to poor but from one generation of the rich to another. Even to talk of a 'top 5 per cent' is imprecise and misleading. The summit is reached by few; the top 5 per cent includes at its bottom reaches people with quite modest savings. Since the wealthy are also those who benefit most from inflation, the wave of new fortunes made in Britain on land and property have, if anything, increased the inequities.

When it reaches such proportions, the lopsidedness of society has insidious chain-reactions. The poorest in Britain have the worst diets: they buy 13 per cent less milk than average, 16 per cent less meat, 5 per cent fewer eggs. In turn, the deficiencies of diet increase the incidence of sickness, and yet the National Health Service spends one-third more on treatment for the richest than on the poorest.

Public housing subsidizes a working-class family's rent to an average of £18 a year, but the tax relief on loans for those able to buy their own homes runs at an average of £62 a year. Because their children stay at school longer and have more chance of reaching university, a family making £4,000 a year can reckon to cost the state half as much again as the national average. Even then, only one in eight of British children between the ages of 20 and 24 is at university. The Welfare State has been warped so that it reflects and supports the bias in favour of rich against poor. In Britain over the few years between the mid-'sixties and early 'seventies about 100 people made as much money on property speculation as it would take the average worker 2,000 years to earn.

There is no discernible sense of outrage at this state of affairs. Things have been run this way for so long that the poor are as fatalistic as the rich are intransigent. In all the other industrial democracies, the original lucre of capitalism has been ground into dust and dispersed (save, of course, for the more resilient dynasties) to the point where, as in the U.S.A., and France, and Germany, middle-class wealth represents social equilibrium. This has happened, to the chagrin of Marxists, without requiring the dissolution of capitalism. In Britain, in possibly the most sustained act of deception and organized cupidity since Carthage, the fruits due to the many have been retained by the few.

A curious quirk of the British *psyche* is that, instead of being provoked to fury by the continued injustices of their system, the people direct their resentments anywhere but at that system. Perhaps this is why the system has survived for so long – by providing decoys. As they sink into the trance of True Brit, the British seem to think that the cause of their hard times lies somewhere else, probably with foreigners. The fusion in the British soul of pride of heritage, ethnic *hauteur*, sanctimony, and totem-worship easily turns into a sour resentment of old enemies and newly risen competitors.

Joining the European Common Market has increased rather than diminished these tensions. Forcing the British into Europe was, in any case, an act of desperation. For more than ten years, three British Prime Ministers tried to recover from the initial blunder made when Anglo–Saxon condescension rejected the chance of signing the Treaty of Rome on the formation of the Common Market. Later, the idealism of a united Europe took on for the British a more urgent and expedient purpose. With the economy permanently convalescent, the pound sterling ebbing away, and endemic industrial unrest, Europe seemed to offer a draconian remedy – disciplines that couldn't be imposed from the inside would be inescapable with the country opened up to full-blooded competition.

This has never been conceded as a motive, but it had compulsive attraction for politicians, Harold Wilson as much as Edward Heath. There was no other trick left to try – unless, of course, they were to do something radical about the basic inequities of wealth which were as responsible as anything for the economic shambles of the country. But that would have been unthinkable.

To the rest of Europe, the British look like somebody staggering home, slightly tipsy, from a fancy-dress ball, still absurdly costumed and in his mind still living the part he is dressed up for. As this bizarre figure knocks on the door to beg admittance, it blinks in the unwelcome light of reality and turns surly and regretful that the dream is ended. Strutting, posing and posturing, vain and patronizing, the apparition has the brittle charm of an ageing Thespian – sometimes to be pitied, sometimes exasperating, occasionally droll. Britain is a victim of time-warp, promising to reform but really not grasping either the extent of her waywardness or the means of curing it.

The British advocates of the new Europe have tried to make up for the revolution that Britain never had. The gift of gradualism, so frequently paraded as the anchor of the country's stability, has really been its undoing. Although it is the last kind of lesson the British are ready to learn, the clue to the real cause of their strangled society lies in the fields of France. France was shaped (or rather not shaped) by the French Revolution; Britain has been shaped, in both the physical and social sense, by the Industrial Revolution.

The British conception of France as a nation of blue-smocked peasants has at one and the same time seen the point and missed it. France was originally industrialized not at the expense of the peasantry: the rural communities of France stayed in possession of their land. Wealth in land, wealth from industry, the wealth of the *rentier* in the towns, and finally the affluence of the new middle class, progressed in parallel in France, without any one of these groups having to give way to another. In the end this has built a spread of prosperity, in significant contrast to the polarized wealth of the British.

British capitalism and the Industrial Revolution did not coincide. The pocketing of wealth by the few had already taken place before the first mechanized spinning-wheel marked the end of cottage industries and the dawn of mass production. It was the dissipation and venality of the Tudor monarchy that set the pattern for stripping the country of its wealth. By the time of Henry VIII, the families from the British shires who schemed in the royal court were grabbing thousands of acres of land. More than a quarter of England was in the hands of a new landowning aristocracy. Another quarter, perhaps more, was in the hands of the Church, as much a political and capitalist enterprise as a spiritual one. The Church also collected 30 per cent of the customary dues paid by the smaller landowners to the greater.

With the Crown increasingly desperate for money to raise armies and to defend itself, it turned on the Church and gave dispensation to the landowners to grab Church lands. By the early seventeenth century more than half of the land was in the hands of a powerful oligarchy of plundering landowners. The monarchy itself was impoverished, already decaying into a symbol and tool. The people of

England had been dispossessed of what was then the only universal prospect of wealth and security: land and property.

The appropriation of this wealth was completed just as Newcomen built his steam engine; within another generation Hargreaves had produced the spinning jenny, James Watt his condenser patent. Iron ore had been smelted by coke. All these innovations needed capital: and the source of capital lay with the landowning oligarchy, families whose wealth was less than a century old. During that decisive first impact of future shock, there were incredible tides running: the Puritans recoiled from the mercenary orgy and went off to make their New England; paper money and modern banking were devised; the English peasantry were coerced into industrial slavery; technology was the new witchcraft; Adam Smith wrote *The Wealth of Nations*. And the British were defeated in the American Revolution.

The world changed, but not the inherent imbalance of wealth in Britain. No wonder the British ruling classes abhorred the French Revolution and reviled Bonaparte. An alternative idea was planted in Europe, and although it took nearly 200 years to do so it has finally led to the humiliation of the British: an economic humiliation rather than a military one.

Now, in their ethnocentricity, the British suspect that European membership is the beginning of racial pollution, a subtler variety than they had already been asked to endure by living alongside their black slaves. One survey of British attitudes towards Europe turned up a pronounced aversion to the bidet, which is thought of as 'dirty' and 'Continental'. Although the British are reticent on the subject, it appears that the average Briton takes a bath only once every three days.

In the British view of Europe, food seems crucial. The liberal middle class, who are mostly pro-European, have tasted French food and can't wait to see the grisly diet of the British pub replaced by the delights of the Paris bistro. The conservative working class, on the other hand, who are heavily anti-European, are deeply suspicious of anything other than their own bland and greasy diet.

A year after the British had, in theory, become fully paid-up Europeans they were more hostile to the idea rather than less. Ironically, the greatest suspicion of and hostility towards Europeans comes from the poorest and the oldest among the British. They do not seem to realize that of all the European democracies, the one that screws them the most is their own. It is not the Common Market that made the British the paupers of Europe.

'Mr Hughes looks on Britain as an English-speaking
country with good communications, relatively free of
bureaucracy, and somewhere that will afford him
privacy.' – anonymous spokesman for Howard Hughes

Having been dislodged by an earthquake in Central America,
and fast running out of sympathetic accommodations, the
millionaire settled into a floor at the Inn on the Park in
London. The demands of a recluse are peculiar but not
extensive. A darkened room in Mayfair is much like a darkened room anywhere. But that capsule summary of the
British virtues, although a trifle contrived, did make people
feel that the place still had something to offer for the more
fastidious tastes. There are some people, though, for whom
there can be too much civilization. S. J. Perelman, for
example: 'English life, while very pleasant, is rather bland.
I expected kindness and gentility and I found it, but there
is such a thing as too much couth.' This was disappointing.
As a life-long Anglophile, Perelman had sold his house in
New York State, spat on New York City as a pestilence
to be discarded, and set out to do everything required to be
an English gentleman. He had even joined the Reform Club.
A year later he was back in the most depraved quarter of
New York City, seeking out his old delicatessen. Apart from
being too bland, London had not been able to provide rolls
with sesame seed.

Like many another Anglophile, Perelman had been
chasing moonbeams. The England he imagined, and the one
he had so affectionately created in short stories, had never

really existed. Phileas Fogg had never belonged to the Reform Club; he had been invented by a Frenchman. A man who behaved like Fogg would never be allowed in the company of gentlemen. He was not bland enough.

> Englishmen in Knightsbridge today stuck to their stiff upperlip tradition. When they saw a young man running naked down the pavement and across the busy road they averted their eyes. The man, aged about 30, was completely starkers, but he barely [sic] raised an eyebrow from many early morning shoppers and businessmen. It was only when a motor-cycle policeman stopped that a crowd began to stare. The policeman chased the naked man across the road and finally caught him on the corner of Knightsbridge and Sloane Street. A raincoat was hastily thrown over him as he lay on the pavement. – Item in the London *Evening Standard*.

Averting the gaze from the naked truth sounds amusing enough in this context, but – as Perelman said – you can have such a thing as too much couth. One of the reasons why commercial, political and social dirty tricks pass undetected in Britain is that it is thought to be unseemly to look for them. A great deal of reliance can be placed on this fine sensibility by people who lack scruple but share, for obvious reasons, the code of discretion. Such cool makes the British feel superior: 'Naturally the British do not, among the nations, have a monopoly of good manners; but they are bringing a valuable asset to add to the existing stock of European codes of conduct.' – the *Sunday Times*.

It is doubtful whether the Europeans share this euphoric view of the more abstract qualities which the British took with them into the Common Market. Within months of their admittance, a B.B.C. correspondent reported that, having thought the phrase 'perfidious Albion' might now be buried for ever, he had heard or read it three or four times in the past three months. Furthermore, the British delegation had been, he said, falling rather short of that 'existing stock of European codes of conduct' – ' ... their behaviour at the European Parliament has been described to me as that of "men discovering with delight that Britain's Indian Empire never really died".' Even before the British proconsuls had crossed the channel, a survey conducted by the scholarly British journal *New Society* turned up a surprising quirk of national racial prejudice: 'It showed how, even among people who said they were pro-Marketeers, there was much more human sympathy with the Americans (or with Nigerians) than with the French.' British reserves of 'human sympathy' are, in any case, carefully conserved. They were never generous. The Americans and the Nigerians can consider themselves especially favoured. As for the French, well, they would certainly return the compliment. It is hard to love a country which has twice in one century had to help save you from the Germans – and from yourselves. Building an affection for the English, if you aren't a natural Anglophile, is difficult for anybody, as the author and critic Anthony Burgess confessed:

> The impossibility of anybody's really liking the English (or, by colonial extension, the Americans either) is demonstrated again and again. The world's hope for the English, if it has one, certainly the Englishman's hope for himself, if he has one, lies in that old eagerness to teach, which, perhaps by definition, has nothing to do with being simpatico.

Well, nobody likes or loves a pedagogue, least of all a British pedagogue. But what is it that the British have left to teach other people? Integrity, perhaps? 'Only one leading democracy, Britain, has remained comparatively unspotted. The famous Profumo affair, a few years ago, astounded the British not because it disclosed a gaudy private life in higher political echelons but because a junior minister lied to the House of Commons.' – C. L. Sulzberger, *International Herald Tribune.*

Not so, and no marks for prescience: not long after this

fashionable wisdom was penned, Lord Lambton followed Profumo into malodour for the same taste in private pleasure, give or take an extra partner, and although he confessed with celerity he was summarily despatched. The real offence was coupling beneath his station. No lady arranges for photos to be taken through a two-way mirror. It was no use Lambton saying that he did it for 'variety'. He was slumming, and that one simply must not do.

And another thing. That spotless democracy of Cyrus Sulzberger's – so indispensable to the editorial writers of the *New York Times* every time they want to cast a shadow over their own system – is an illusion. In Britain minor corruption is passed off by using the quaint term 'fiddling'. But attitudes towards 'fiddling' are complicated by that other British vice, class prejudice. As the B.B.C. magazine *The Listener* recorded: 'According to an anthropologist, Gerald Mars, waiters, fairground workers, dustmen, dockers and many another proletarian Uncle Tom Cobley are on the fiddle: it's often thought a legitimate part of their pay. But the middle classes fiddle too, though they look on working-class fiddles with horror.' Fiddling is nourished in the favourable, secretive climate of local government; in effect local politics has become big business, with one sixth of the British gross national product flowing through the hands of councils. An ex-Mayor in the north, gaoled in a case involving £6,700 in bribes paid to secure building contracts, said that backhanders were the 'normal run of the mill'. And that, as the judge observed, seemed to be only the tip of the iceberg. But the Anglophiles of the *New York Times* will have none of it. The more depraved their own political system became, the more dependent they were on the preservation of British virginity. The paper's most addicted upholder of British virtue, Anthony Lewis, considered the political crime of Watergate to be beyond British comprehension: 'Misuse of power on so enormous a scale is simply unimaginable here. Because they do not appreciate the occasion for it, some Britons cannot understand the public method of the Senate committee's proceedings. The correctives here are quiet and internal.' Which was, though he appeared not to know it, another way of saying that in Britain the cover-up is a tidy and highly refined art. Under the law of contempt of court, as soon as the smallest fish is caught all the fat cats who feed off him are assured that reporters will be silenced. Sacrificial offerings are made of those dumb enough to be caught, while the rest who know the rules of the game better lie low until it is safe to play again. There may well be a difference of degree between British and American 'fiddling', but the corruption of ethic is identical.

And even the most hallowed symbols of patriotism are not immune to it: the Royal Navy, bulwark of Britannia, was caught with its hand in the cash-box. Seventy-five naval officers and ratings were convicted of taking bribes paid by firms supplying food to navy messes. Although a swindle costing £110,000 was nailed, the police estimated that the real sum had been more like £500,000: 'This type of crime in the navy stretches back over years and years, and the total stolen must run into millions of pounds,' said a detective. Time after time that ubiquitous phrase 'the tip of the iceberg' is used. The truth is that British cool keeps icebergs well under the waves.

Anglophiles serve only to keep the British firm in their hypocrisy. The incorrigible Anthony Lewis again: 'Americans especially notice the difference (in Britain) from their own Galbraithian balance of private affluence and public squalor.' Which sat awkwardly in contrast to this: 'Three hundred people may die from cold on Christmas Day in Britain, the Young Liberals declared yesterday. The movement was launching a campaign to focus public attention on hypothermia, the hidden killer.' – item in the London *Times*, December 19th, 1972. During that season of good cheer, one old woman had been found dead in her home after eating cardboard in an effort to keep warm. An organization called 'Age Concern' was formed to provide a voluntary emergency service.

But not even bombers could shake Lewis from his reverie. On the day that I.R.A. bombs killed one man and injured 200 people in central London, he was walking along the Thames embankment filled with the joys of spring, and a good lunch: ' ... exquisite crocuses were in bloom, yellow and purple and white. A country that still cares about flowers, I thought ... ' In the country that still cared about flowers, the government subsidizes mining companies to drill for minerals in the National Parks; resort towns discharge sewage into the ocean; remote islands which have resisted two hundred years of industrialization are being appropriated for oil refineries; unpoliced factories pour sulphur dioxide into the air and lethal chemicals into the rivers. No wonder, then, that on such a deep tradition of hypocrisy the native pundits should themselves be in confusion about the state of the nation:

> Britain is still the best country in the world for her citizens or her visitors. Democratic, tolerant, good natured, skilled, resourceful and in some ways determined in her people, beautiful in her countryside and cultivated in her cities, Britain is still a nation to be envied. – *The Times*, October 30th, 1972

> British society is in a number of respects less cohesive than it was. Class divisions may be less conspicuous than in previous generations. Differences in income may matter less than they did, not because the position of the poor has been relatively improved but because with the general rise in prosperity more satisfactions are brought within everyone's grasp. But British society has become more atomized. There is a less clear sense of identity. The feeling of being part of a wider community is no longer so pronounced. – *The Times*, a month later.

Some countries gain a sense of security from the will to change, the drive to improve. The British sense of security is precariously dependent on an opposite concept: the *status quo*. Keeping things as they are has an important motive: it keeps people where they are. Fear in one section of the community that their position is being eroded by another group is deeply founded: despite frequent gestures towards 'levelling-up' most of the channels of privilege have survived. The upper classes resent the *nouveau riche*; the middle classes consolidate their own continuity; the working class has the satisfaction of having another even less privileged class to push around: the blacks. One group rides on the backs of the other. In a society where 'progress' means basically one class succeeding at the expense of another, 'egalitarianism' has joined all the other myths to become, perhaps, the most dangerous of all. The longer it persists, the more divisive will be its final exposure. A series of tensions has been set up which run through British life. It is not so clearly drawn as the old class war: things have diffused into a cluster of separate conflicts involving class, ethics, morals, ideologies. The apparent coherence of Britain is an illusion.

4 *The Importance of Clubmanship*

Britain is run through an extensive network of private transactions. It is the most secretive ruling system in the western
world. The British invented the gentlemen's club, and
variations of the club principle are indispensable to the
clandestine power networks. The visible and acknowledged
clubs play a part in this process, but more important are the
looser and more shadowy aggregations of vested interests
and influence peddling.

The principle of the club is the key to understanding
how British society preserves its continuity. While the more
flagrant superstructure of the class system apparently disappeared, it had merely gone underground. The club is an
underground circuit. If clubs hadn't already been invented
they would have had to come into being sooner or later.
Today Britain is riddled with clubs. They range from the
powerful to the powerless. At their most opaque they contain enormous influence.

The club is a cross between a tribal cell and a secret
society. It is a game anybody can play: if you're an outsider
to one club you can be an insider to the next. This game
appeals to the British because it is a progressively elitist
process. Clubs provide a perfect cover for discrimination.
From the bottom to the top each group becomes smaller
until, at the very top, it is at its most discriminating. The
British form into clubs as fish form into shoals, as sheep into
flocks, as Sicilians into families. Like the Mafia, the really
important clubs have no formal shape. Of them all, there
are three which, in descending order, cover the country's
affairs:

The Custodians

In this supposedly model democracy, the country is not run by the people elected to run it. The power of Parliament has been systematically eroded; real power lies elsewhere in the hands of the Custodians.

This elusive entity is more extensive than the old concept of the 'Establishment'. It outlives governments and fashions in politics. It is not only unelected but it is self-recruiting and self-sustaining.

A prime function of the Custodians is to preserve True Brit; True Brit created them and without it they would perish. Behind every convulsion of this agonized country they stand as the last line of the *status quo*. Change can come only on their terms, and to their advantage. The secret of their potency is continuity: twenty-five years of social flux have done nothing to disturb their tenancy. They are the wall on which every tide breaks and turns.

And yet the Custodians do not behave like an organized conspiracy. That would be too unsubtle. They have no formal mass. Their influence permeates the country from top to bottom, but it is never finite. Like amoebae they have no constant shape. Their intercourse is mysterious. They cluster, separate, and cluster again. The only link is the habit of the club.

Along Pall Mall and in St James's are the clubs that form the epicentre of the Custodians' world: the Athenaeum, the Travellers, the Carlton, Brooks's, White's. Many of their transactions are made here. This is the switchboard through which the messages come. But even then it is only the most evident part. There are other outposts: All Souls' at Oxford, a few other colleges, other cells. But then the tracks begin to disappear into the undergrowth, weaving to the discreetest outpost of power and influence.

This network was woven long ago, for the convenience of a ruling elite. It was a part of the system which was supposed to collapse under new social pressures. But its resilience has been seriously underestimated. The Custodians now seem rather like one of those extra-terrestrial invading armies in a science-fiction movie: every instrument of earthly resistance has been unleashed on them, the ground is thick with the smoke of battle, and then out of it all materializes the enemy, unscathed. But in their case the extraordinary truth is that their survival was a fortuitous accident.

When the country withdrew from Empire it had to find a substitute role. If it had been susceptible to reality it would have sought not just a new role, but one which was in line with its diminished power. This was too much to ask of the British. The new course they chose was viable enough, but they immediately equated it with the old glories and were therefore doomed to overreach themselves. The national ego was redirected towards business. Massive commitments were made to industrial and commercial growth. But the implications of this redirection were not grasped.

In particular, there were three ways in which this change was in collision with the national character: socially, ethically and technically. Socially the profit motive was taboo; you could believe in it, pursue it, and prosper by it, but you didn't talk about it. The ethical conflict flowed from this: by its new standards, the country required that the making of money should be an acceptable motivation in its own right, just as imperial conquest had once been. The technical problem was one of habit: the two other problems were matters of character, while this was a matter of competence. Technical competence had never been highly valued, and consequently it wasn't in conspicuous supply.

Since there was no new body of competent men to turn to for the direction of the country's chosen role, the old one had to suffice. As it happened, this suited the Custodians perfectly. In the preparation of the corporate state, the process of management was heavy in mystique. The problems were conveniently abstruse, and the projects far too prolonged to fit neatly into the lifespan of one government. If they could appropriate the right to run these projects they would, in effect, be running the country. After a series of devious manoeuvres that is just what they did.

As Britain's power slides from the first to second rank, and then to third, the power of the Custodians is at its height. There is, perhaps, a fatal law in this, like the mating of the sockeye salmon. The journey upstream, against the odds, is fulfilled in one great orgasm; and then come decay and death. True Brit has that kind of obsessive quality.

The League of Gentlemen

Bertrand Russell said that the 'gentleman' was invented to symbolize the claims to power of a mixed class of aristocrats and industrialists. But the rank of 'gentleman' has always been secondary; gentlemen are not the elite in Britain. The Custodians are the embodiment of the mystique of 'the finest minds'. Their whole ethos is intellectual. The terms of membership for the League of Gentlemen are far laxer. They depend not so much on substance as on appearance. The qualifications lend themselves easily to counterfeit. The League of Gentlemen is full of fakes.

And yet the strange thing is that money alone cannot buy membership. Manner and style are everything. Without them, money is dirt. The Custodians hold the power of the state, the League of Gentlemen hold the power of business.

In the British corporate state a great deal was expected of the League of Gentlemen: they were supposed to provide the officer class of the new mercantile army. But it is now painfully clear that the qualities required of the gentleman are not those required of a modern business manager. The gentleman is self-centred, not corporation-motivated nor noticeably loyal to the national interest. His prime concern is his own welfare. In order to follow this light he has enjoyed a laxity of ethics unique in any business community.

A common myth about the gentleman is that he has scruple. As many who have had dealings with gentlemen will testify, they can be the most unscrupulous operators in the world. They are so plausible. There is their unwritten

code – 'the gentleman's agreement', 'the word of a gentleman is his bond'. It has taken them far. But the cards are
marked. It takes a gentleman to spot a gentleman: all others
beware.

The gentleman is not much liked by the Custodians. To
them business is a grubby trade; they are not – as will be
amply evident – at their best in dealing with it. The gentleman finds his self-esteem not by looking up, but by looking
down. He discriminates against non-gentlemen with ruthless
contempt. In London after World War I society was so
depleted by the carnage of the battlefield that, for a while,
interlopers from below were allowed. They were called
'temporary gentlemen'. Once the bloodstock was replen-
ished, out they went.

Gentlemen believe in True Brit. They should. It has
provided their featherbed. They have been the factors of
True Brit, trading on its bogus virtues in many a gullible
market place. They do not like the new sales resistance to
True Brit, the many signs that in itself it is no longer enough.
Even at home there are rumblings of discontent. But one of
the planks of the gentleman's ego is that he believes the
world owes him a living. Just as it owes respect to True Brit.
He cannot grasp that his game is being called.

The gentleman's ability to survive depends more and
more on the defences of his club, the City of London. The
gentlemen have had to close their ranks to remain secure.
Like any body of men under siege, they have to be careful
whom they allow through the City gates, lest there be sab-
oteurs among them. They have been reinforced by some
new money which has proved acceptable. The oil business,
for example, needs men of style and cunning, and since
suave manipulation is a mark of the gentleman he has done
well in oil.

But the gentlemen have been sorely provoked by men
who come from no club, and who show no respect for the
codes of the club system. This has been a new and disconcerting experience in the City of London, a lawless place

that frowns on innovations in lawlessness. The Hustlers have come to town, skilfully exploiting its soft spots and making a great deal of money at other people's expense. Harsh things have been said, and the barricades have been reinforced.

The Fiddlers

The Fiddlers are the outsiders who created their own inside. Excluded by both the Custodians and the League of Gentlemen, the Fiddlers could follow suit in one way: they got organized. From the Custodians they learned the value of clandestine power. They have taken their own slice of territory: local government. And from the League of Gentlemen they took an ethical lead: do anything as long as you don't get caught.

The Fiddlers are the newest and most disconcerting of the clubs. Disconcerting, because they have shaken to its roots one of the last remaining myths of the British system – the picture of a selfless, industrious and scrupulously honest grassroots political fabric. In fact, the Fiddlers have come from that section of British society which was screwed by the League of Gentlemen for 200 years. They spring from the clerical and trading classes, who served silently for so long while the fruits were picked by gentlemen. The Fiddlers had a ready-made social network, clubs with charitable intent like the Rotarians, or slightly bizarre rituals, like the Freemasons. They also used to be God-fearing Anglicans, Wesleyans, Episcopalians, Methodists. But suddenly they got the message that the man who preached on Sunday fiddled on Monday. As middle-class venality became more blatant, the outsiders wanted to be in.

Their chance came almost by accident. All corrupt systems have to have a source of temptation. Until recently temptation in large amounts was noticeably lacking from British local politics. The authorities had been starved of funds, the machine run on a shoestring. Then, in the early 1960s, huge sums were pumped into the coffers of the legislators to fund regional rebuilding programmes. City politicians had a new power: architectural patronage. And they quickly learned the value of that patronage.

Contracts for new hospitals, schools, offices, city centres and housing developments were the stuff that graft was made of. Much of the fiddling was small, operated within a cosy local fellowship in which politics, business and social life overlapped with ease and discretion. Some of it escalated into wider, regional fellowships.

The more parochial the fiddling is, the better its protection. On that scale it fits snugly into familiar and matured circuits. The Fiddlers do not like people who get too big for their boots. Security lies in modesty. Fiddlers do not bother with True Brit: it is too blatant for their taste and they leave it to the gentlemen. True Brit touches their lives in only one way: Fiddlers are good monarchists.

5

The Custodians:
Men of Power, Feet of Clay

The night train from the north pulls into London. From a sleeper a small, assertive-looking red-haired woman emerges. The men standing by the black limousine spot her at once. There are a few hurried words. Two of the men fall into step beside the woman, overshadowing her. Together they pile into the car, which slips out into the early morning city traffic. The two men, now attached like bodyguards, follow the redhead into her apartment. A startled man, her husband, sits up bleary-eyed in bed as the trio walks in. 'Darling,' the redhead says, 'here's my Private Secretary and my Chief Information Officer.' She takes a bath; the three men have tea in the kitchen.

A connexion has been made which will occupy every waking minute of the woman's life.

It sounds like a scene from an espionage movie. In fact, the woman has been pulled off a north-bound train in the middle of the night to take a phone call from the Prime Minister. He wants to switch her from one government department to another. She agrees, but she has to head back to town to be 'inducted'. From the second she leaves that train she is virtually in the custody of the shadowy eminences who are in theory her servants but who are, in reality, the Custodians. They move like a screen between the minister and the world. The myth that politicians run the country founders on these men. They run the politicians.

In this instance, the contrast between the political appearance and the political reality is astonishing. The redhead is the Labour-party firebrand Barbara Castle, who told her story, more in sorrow than in anger, to a conference of civil servants. There is behind her a lifetime of party-political experience, a record of adroit in-fighting and passionate left-wing convictions. She has a quick, sure intellect. Once she was even thought of as perhaps the first woman Prime Minister.

But the Custodians move in. The tigress is tamed, or smothered. Afterwards she recalls 'The Minister is alone: the loneliness of the short-distance runner ... the administrator will always win, for the simple reason that he knows the ropes.'

A slightly untidy, donnish man is talking, and he is also reflecting on power, and how it evaded him: 'I knew there was this inner committee of Permanent Secretaries. The basic economic strategy of the Government was being planned by this collection of civil servants. How rarely could we ever have a discussion in the Cabinet without it virtually having been made a *fait accompli* by the previous decisions behind the scenes ... '

This time the speaker is Richard Crossman interviewed on B.B.C. television; like Barbara Castle an ex-minister in the government of Harold Wilson, left-wing intellectual, party theoretician. He, too, was neutralized by the Custodians, or – his own words – 'put into a Whitehall cocoon'.

The pattern was consistent, and it went right to the top. Marcia Williams, Wilson's own personal secretary, revealed in her memoirs that her master had been under the thumb of the Civil Service. He was, she said, 'a civil servant *manqué*' – so bewitched by the mystique of the Custodians that they played on his ego and had their way.

Wilson may have been unwarily impressionable, but the mystique is a powerful one. To a large extent it depends for its effect on the cult of the 'fine mind'. The word 'mandarin' is used to recall the old Chinese elite, the nine grades of rigorously selected officials. As Ian Fleming glamourized the essentially seedy British Secret Service, the Civil Service has been portrayed as a race of intellectual supermen by the novels of C. P. Snow. There is a common trick: both make literary capital out of arcane crafts, allowing great scope for the imagination. Take this passage from *Corridors of Power*, Snow's 1964 novel about Whitehall, in which he describes his quintessential mandarin, Hector Rose: 'They had given him the Grand Cross of the Bath, the sort of decoration he and his friends prized, but which no one else noticed. He still worked with the precision of a computer ... he did his duty, and a good deal more than his duty.'

Snow's inspiration as a novelist is similar to that of many journalists. He is a power-*voyeur*. Just as Fleming made espionage titillating, Snow makes Whitehall into an arena for combat of a kind closely linked to the libido: the struggle for the mastery of the Executive. There are a couple of lines in Snow's novel *Homecomings* which gave a direct stimulus to those who wanted to hold the Custodians in awe: ' ... as the war went on and the state became more interleaved with business, civil servants like Rose had made themselves tougher minded ... '.

In the 1960s, these 'tougher-minded' civil servants seemed to crop up all over, essential figures in the scenario of the glamourized Whitehall ... the Gods of True Brit. In one thing at least, Snow was sentient. At the end of the 1950s, as the most visible champion of the new technocracy, he formulated his famous Harvard lectures on 'The Two Cultures' – science versus the arts. Far more than he could realize, the tension between these two forces gave the Custodians both a massive extension of their influence and, at the same time, provided the ground on which their mythological competence would come to grief.

Their Achilles heel is the way the Custodians select their own kind – the educational channel from which they are drawn. This covers not only those of the Custodians who end up in Whitehall, but also those who fill the club's other annexes: the Foreign Service, the Judiciary, and the academic outposts which harbour 'advisers' and institutional carpet-baggers.

Within Whitehall, the central cell of the Custodians, the power balance has switched from favouring the old pro-consulate of empire, in the Foreign Office, to the domestic departments. The profession of the civilized amateur survived in the colonies, but the demands of contemporary Britain were too much for it. The animal cannot adapt. The social, cultural, and educational conditioning of the Custodians have left them stranded in an unfamiliar and taxing world. They are the products of a selective process which has been selecting the wrong talent. The heart of this process is a conduit of the highest-ranking public schools – Eton, Harrow, Winchester – and the colleges of Oxford and Cambridge.

This conduit is not the exclusive preserve of the Custodians; they cream off the top candidates and let the rest find their level in the League of Gentlemen which, at its junkier fringe, also takes in the duds from the second-rate public schools and, if they get that far, Oxbridge and lesser universities. The mandatory ingredients of the civilized amateur, if he is to make it into the Custodians, are that inimitable *persona*, George Sanders without the charm, and the Greek culture rather than the Roman. The segregation built into this elitist conduit has been proof against all social adulteration; it is as biased now towards privilege as ever it was. True Brit demands it.

Oxbridge is not only a source of higher education. It is the final filter for membership of the Custodians. It reflects in microcosm the values and *mores* which will govern the mature attitudes of those inducted into it. A strong psychological necessity is a feeling of superiority – not only social superiority but vocational superiority. At Oxbridge the contacts with the scouting system of the Custodians are highly developed. The first taste a man gets of the informality of the process – a chance meeting here, a nod there, the development of a family connexion, the social intercourse in which character is assessed in the most casual circumstances – show its style. To the right man, who will by dint of his earlier social conditioning find this a natural development and be at ease within it, the possibilities are great. To an undergraduate from a different social background, up from a state school or from a lesser public school and without both the connexions and the social graces, the concept of equal opportunity begins to seem illusory.

This is the dividing line: despite the lip-service to equality of opportunity, the network of privilege has survived and adapted. Oxbridge sorts out the Custodians from the gentlemen. The inductees see that this is the way business should work, a fluid mating of ambition and opportunity, the 'oral interview' with the putative character being probed for the blemish of excess: too much zeal, too much lip, too much idealism. They must also show the negative qualities, because it is axiomatic to the Custodians that they must preserve True Brit by stopping things as much as by starting them. An elegant style in inertia is highly valued. It will be the benchmark of higher rank. As one ex-mandarin puts it: 'The average official would rather miss a dozen opportunities than make one mistake.'

For all its discrimination, the selection filter of the Custodians can sometimes be disastrously indiscriminate. The unspoken and unwritten criteria depend implicitly on *laxity*: if a man passes muster by looking and sounding right it is against the code to delve beyond the satisfactory veneer. If he looks wrong in the superficial things, if the diction is coarse at the edge, then his character will be pressed. If not, not.

This is the innate consent of clubmanship. Its most conspicuous disaster, one which left the process wounded but not over-repentant, was the case of the three spies, Guy Burgess, Donald Maclean, and Kim Philby. They were all at Cambridge in the early 1930s, though not visibly linked. Burgess, loose, Bohemian and homosexual, was none the less an old Etonian and had enough swagger to recover from dissipation and make it into British Intelligence by social

manipulation, and via *The Times* and the B.B.C. On the way
he made an attempt to work for the Tory party's research
department, abortive when his prospective employer complained: 'But what about his *nails*?' Maclean, epicene but
more personable, breezed into the diplomatic corps. Philby,
the son of a proconsul who had managed both to belong to
the Athenaeum and be a Muslim with two wives, was less
flamboyant than his father and ingratiated himself so effectively with the Custodians that he worked, at increasingly
high levels, in the British Secret Service for three decades.

This trinity of dissemblers, plausible enough by background to get easily through the elitist filter, were all Soviet
agents. When Burgess and Maclean defected to their
masters it ruptured relations between the British and the
C.I.A.; when Philby, the consummate double agent, capped
his career with a passage to Moscow it left the Americans
speechless. But that is not the end. There were two re-
cruiting systems at work at Cambridge in the 1930s: the
Custodians' and the Russians'. Whoever it was who saw
through the veneer of these three into their treacherous
hearts still, for all we know, sits in some corner of a London
club among his fellows and muses on the certainty of his
eye for talent. And if that was the most spectacular breach
of the system, what other warps of mind and body have
slipped through, malign or merely incompetent, to complete
another shorted circuit? It is quite a thought.

It will be said that things don't work that way any more.
Then consider this. The middle and upper ranks of the
Custodians are now the crop of the period between 1948 and
1960. And there is a salient bias in this generation that makes
it unique. It contains by far the lowest proportion of en-
trants with mathematics or science degrees this century –
just 4 per cent. (It was 25 per cent between 1905 and 1914,
and sank to 12 per cent by 1937.) This means that 96 per
cent of the leadership in Whitehall has the classic arts background of the civilized amateur. They are Greeks wrestling
with the Roman world.

Correcting an error like this is like taking the wheel of a 200,000-ton oil tanker and trying to avoid a rock a few hundred yards ahead. It can't be done. A change made now would take until 1990 to work through.

This cultural bias is really a benign corruption: the top 2 or 3 per cent of the country's brains are the wrong kind of brains. The reason is that the social matrix is not the professional one; it doesn't match. The mould of True Brit emphasizes that light assurance of social superiority rather than the less respected but now indispensable training of the sciences. To the mind of the Custodian, the skills of management are rude and grubby: they connect to reality, they defy flights of philosophy. The Custodian cannot grasp the redundancy of his training, or that his blood line has been rendered extinct, along with so many of the traits of True Brit. When he is forced to deal in the jungle of business he is credulous and naïve. He cannot read the play, he cannot do the sums. But nor will he yield his power.

And here is the awful paradox: more omnipotent than ever, and less accountable, the Custodians cannot handle their job. For more than ten years, through an incremental process which they did not initiate, the running of the country has passed further into their hands. It cannot easily be won back. But they fumble from one catastrophe to another, playing their role with an arrogant conviction in spite of the wreckage in their wake.

Her hair is grey now, but the eyes are clear and wise. She, too, has pulled back from the fight, though from the other side. Dame Evelyn Sharp was Richard Crossman's Custodian, reaching an Olympian height for a woman civil servant. But her experience of power has given her pause. Interviewed on B.B.C. television, she said:

Changes in the organization and machinery of our system of government are overdue: some are being made, but not, to my way of thinking, enough, and they are nothing like radical enough. We're much too complacent about our Parliamentary and Ministerial system. The real peril is that we may suddenly become frightened by the way things appear to be going and in our fright look for a more authoritarian form of government – *and there are people waiting in the wings.*

'The Establishment' in its old sense provided a means of identifying a power-collective that was elusive. It did have certain formal routes through which it worked: the courts, the Executive, the institutions. Acting singly and openly through any one of these bases the Established powers could be detected. The value of the term 'Establishment' was as shorthand, to explain covert action by some mysterious will. Thus a scapegoat like Stephen Ward in the Profumo affair could be described, correctly, as the victim of a 'vengeful Establishment', when there was no clearer explanation and when the actual conspirators could not be named. The regressive instinct of a ruling elite could be sensed rather than seen.

There will always be these dark currents of mood running behind the exercise of power in Britain. They can sometimes build up in strength against a change in the tolerances of society until they surge against it in the open. A rare instance of this kind of pressure becoming explicit, rather than showing itself through a series of unexplained repressions, arose from that sexual *cause célèbre*, the trial for obscenity of the underground magazine *Oz*.

Although he moderated the original sentences on appeal, the Lord Chief Justice warned: 'We would like to make it quite clear in general terms that any idea that an offence under the Obscene Publications Act 1959 does not merit a prison sentence should be eradicated. *There will be many cases in future in which a prison sentence is appropriate ...* '. The Bench does not often reveal its sentiments or its intentions like this, nor suggest the pre-judgment of future cases.

As convenient as it is, the use of the label 'the Establishment' to describe any collective act by covert groups is now obsolete. It gained currency when the traditional institutions were still relatively undisturbed by modern pressures. Since then, there has been an extensive redistribution of power in Britain. This has been achieved at the expense of principles and elements which were thought basic to that mystical entity, the British Constitution. It has made power harder to identify. It has created new groupings, coalitions, alliances and concentrations of interests and power outside the experience or understanding of most people in the country. Although these forces are novel, the temper of the power collective is still strongly conservative, even reactionary. It has at heart the most hardening of self-interests, the conservation of wealth and privilege.

The unshaken domination of the public-school and Oxbridge closed circuits spreads far wider than Whitehall, as though all the old outposts of empire have still to be staffed. A survey by Dr David Boyd, an American academic, showed that the judiciary, ambassadors, the Church of England hierarchy, the top brass of the Army, Navy and R.A.F., and the heads of the clearing banks come from the same social background as they did in 1939. Two of the public schools, Eton and Winchester, were so consistent in providing the ruling elite that Dr Boyd said they amounted to 'conspiracies rather than educational establishments'. Regardless of their academic records, public schools are recognized as still being the inside track to power.

'The Establishment' will no longer do as a label because it minimizes the problem. To the older vested social and financial interests has been added a rapacious new one, an Orwellian bureaucratic machine that more and more seems to transcend simple human drives like cupidity and ambition. This is not simply a system, it is a new version of the Terror. The Custodians are not its masters, but its keepers.

6

Ritual as the mark of impotence :
Parliament drowns in words, the monarchy hangs on

When a British institution ceases to work it is not discarded:
function fades into ritual, reality is overtaken by myth. This
kind of metamorphosis is exemplified by the monarchy.
What few people have yet grasped is that Parliament, that
eternal torch of the Anglophile, has followed the monarchy
into illustrious impotence. It is the symbol of democratic
consultation long after it has ceased to exercise any real
power.

A curious by-product of the ritualizing process is that,
once embalmed in this way, an institution earns more
reverence and respect than it enjoyed when effective. Politicians themselves have fallen lower and lower in esteem,
but Parliament as an abstraction is more loved – not for
what it is but for what it represents. It is as though the
mock-Gothic shell of the Palace of Westminster, disembodied from its occupants, has become a temple in which
prayers are offered in the hope of national redemption. The
Custodians have made a eunuch of Parliament, but it is a
case of castration by consent.

The defenders of Parliament are incredibly naïve. And
the struggle has produced some strange bedfellows, none
more seemingly incompatible than Michael Foot, the doctrinaire left-winger, and J. Enoch Powell, the right wing's
favourite politician. Foot says: 'I believe that powerful
forces and powerful people are engaged in trying to destroy
the House of Commons.' The only fault with this statement
is that it predicts something which has already happened.
But what is his answer? The same as Powell's, which is:
'Everything which diminishes true debate on the floor of the

House of Commons strengthens the Executive and weakens Parliament.' Both of them regard rhetoric as a form of magnetic field which, once sustained, automatically repels usurpers. The truth is that Parliament has died in the spell of its own voice.

The procedures and powers of Parliament have ossified over the last hundred years, while the role of the Custodians has been transformed from a clerical to a managerial one of vast scope. Parliament has been talking to itself so much that it has failed to notice its own isolation and impotence. A love of language has never been more fatal, but those who succumb to it really believe in debate as one of the British acts of genius, and that words gracefully mustered and elegantly delivered are better than either action or knowledge. Listen, for example, to Brian Walden, a Labour M.P. When it was suggested to him that expert inquisitorial committees (like the American Senate committees) were the only answer to the acquisitive Custodians, he said that this was the kind of idea put forward by people who 'see politics as a science and prefer it that way. They don't want it as an art.'

It was another outbreak of Lord Snow's clash of the cultures, the Greeks versus the Romans. Art is no answer to Parliament's collapse. The House of Commons, whatever its grander illusions, has a basic purpose. It is supposed to represent the public's concern for the way its money is spent. Government expenditure now runs at £16,000m. a year, and is expected to double within a decade. These funds get only the most perfunctory supervision from Parliament, which is kept in a state of consenting ignorance.

In extending their province, the Custodians have drowned Parliament in paper. In 1938, 935 pages were put on the Statute Book by Parliament. In 1971 it was 2,100 pages. Sir William Armstrong, who as Head of the Home Civil Service feeds legislation into Parliament, admits: 'The mass is so great that an awful lot of it is going to get overlooked by the sheer size of it.' George Cunningham, a former civil servant who is now an M.P., sets out the name of the game more clearly: 'The government is in theory subject to the approval of Parliament. In practice it has no scrutiny from Parliament at all. The legislature is not only totally un-influential but doesn't even try to influence the specific purposes for which money is voted.'

Secrecy about money is obsessive. One government after another has refused to disclose their medium-term expen-diture plans, the allocations that really show a government's priorities. Without seeing such a basic tool of money-management Parliament has negligible influence on policy. This concealment is defended on remarkably specious grounds. One of Edward Heath's ministers, Patrick Jenkin, said that if the government revealed how much it thought incomes would rise, the labour unions would immediately submit claims for wage increases based on the estimates. And, giving away the real motive, he added: 'Parliament cannot become in any sense responsible for policy.'

This is really the voice of the Custodians, with the minis-ter playing the ventriloquist's dummy. Public expenditure is the root of real power in the corporate state: if Parliament has no control over that – and it hasn't – the substance of its role is gone.

The Custodians spend public money like drunken sailors, but their binges are revealed only after the event. Parlia-ment's main whistle-blowing body is the Public Accounts Committee. An Auditor-General with 600 accountants serves this committee, but its reports become inquests, not deterrents. To its questions the Custodians provide pathetic and evasive answers. Essential information can be withheld on the most spurious pretexts. In ten years no detailed in-formation on either expenditure or performance was given to the committee about Concorde, on the grounds of 'com-mercial confidentiality'. No better way of sabotaging a rival power can be imagined than providing it with the means to duplicate the Concorde, as the Russians have found to their cost.

The preference for hindsight (a word frequently used by

the Custodians hauled in front of the Public Accounts Committee) over foresight is devastatingly clear from the disposition of teeth to the 'watchdogs'. Against the P.A.C.'s 600 accountants, the body supposed to audit spending as it happens, the Select Committee on Expenditure, has a staff of barely a dozen. Everything is organized to give the profligate Executive the least amount of trouble.

But the furtive administrators can occasionally be jerked out of their leisurely rhythms. When Parliament insists on a piece of legislation being swiftly implemented, against the preference of the Executive, the Custodians have to yield. But there is a catch. They regard this as 'rushing through', a relative term in Whitehall. Under this kind of pressure things get mysteriously muddled. Sir William Armstrong unguardedly reveals the ploy: 'Frequently Acts of Parliament are passed, then after a little while an Amending Act is brought in, the thing is adapted and adjusted and it seems fairly clear, looking back on it, that perhaps the first one was brought in a little faster than it need have been ... '

In other words, play it our way or else ...

Adapting and adjusting, two seemingly innocent terms full of manipulative promise, are supposed to be the functions of the Parliamentary committees which consider legislation as it is transmuted from Bills to Acts. These committees are contrived to give the appearance of bipartisan consultation. In reality they constitute an empty, time-wasting gesture. The government does whatever it sets out to do, under the impress of the Custodians. For example, in one period when 865 amendments were proposed by ministers to their own legislation, 864 were passed. Of 688 amendments asked for by M.P.s not in the government, 39 were passed. M.P.s are ostensibly chosen for these committees on the grounds of appropriate expertise. But their ideas fall on deaf ears if they conflict with the wishes of the Executive. In at least one case it was literally deaf ears: during the four-and-a-half months' passage of one Bill, a government supporter on the committee wore earplugs throughout the proceedings.

If dissenting M.P.s can make no impression, more clandestine pressures can. As the line between government and business dissolves, lobbying by vested interests using their captive M.P.s, and by more covert ministerial routes, is applied with effect. This is the major reason why both the Labour and Tory parties were reluctant to accept a register open to public scrutiny of all financial and business connexions of M.P.s. Many M.P.s, particularly Tories, are so embroiled in business that Parliament is little more to them than a moonlighting exercise with expedient uses.

The kind of thing that *is* taken seriously in Westminster is the trivia of etiquette. As in this exchange:

Mr Wilson: 'What Mr Heath is saying about the Labour Party is a lie' (loud Conservative protests and Labour cheers).

Mr Heath: 'If Mr Wilson uses unparliamentary language that is a matter for him' (loud interruptions).

When, after deliberation, the Speaker of the House deprecated the use of the word 'lie', Wilson withdrew it and substituted 'a pack of lies'. After further deliberations the Speaker ruled that 'a pack of lies' was also contrary to the established etiquette and should not be used again. Also banned are 'that is a lie', 'he is lying', 'liar', 'deceiving', 'deliberately misleading' and 'a damn lie' – together with 'dog', 'cheeky young pup', 'guttersnipe', 'rat', 'stool-pigeon' and 'swine'.

In earlier days Parliament was more robust and, probably, more honest. It was certainly more effective. The blanding of language shows the greying and more euphemistic preferences of an institution which, like the courts, resorts to dignity as a substitute for virility. Parliament is more and more locked out of its own time by ritual. As Edward du Cann, an unusually realistic Tory, puts it: 'Our procedure over the last hundred years or more has been very largely unchanged. Before we preach to Europe about how it should organize its affairs, we have a special duty to put our own house in order.'

One ritual of which Anglophiles stand in awe is the accountability of ministers to Parliament, the daily 'grilling' in the House of Commons. But this is really a masquerade. The conditions under which questions are put are carefully controlled. Sometimes this amounts to rigging. The accepted convention is that questions can be planted to enable a minister to say something in a reply that he cannot present as an unprovoked statement – a partisan piece of boasting, for example. This pretence came unstuck in a case where Julian Amery, the Housing Minister, fed two dozen 'questions' to tame supporters to block an attack by the Opposition. The dummy questions were drafted by civil servants, not even the minister. When these dirty tricks were revealed in *The Sunday Times*, the official response was a pious statement about 'impropriety'.

Another sham procedure is the 'lobby' system. This requires journalists to cover events that never happen. Reporters accredited to the Westminster 'lobby' agree to attend briefings on the basis that they are 'non-attributable' and 'off the record'. This is often used by politicians for kite-flying to test public opinion on a policy. British journalists are content with the servility of this function; they believe that they need the politicians more than the politicians need them, an idea that would be novel in Washington. These tame dogs take their scraps at feeding-time and wag their tails gratefully – unless something goes wrong. When Maurice Macmillan planted a story by this means he saw it faithfully splashed over the front pages of several papers. But the 'leak' misfired (it had mis-stated government policy). Macmillan had to sit silently by as Edward Heath denied that any briefing had taken place. The dogs yelped, but they soon subsided into compliance.

All the lesser deceits amplify the major one – that what happens in the House of Commons has real meaning. The Mother of Parliaments is in her dotage, complacent and impotent. Ironically, Parliament seen purely as an abstraction is, like the monarchy, rated high in the public esteem while the M.P.s themselves have slipped badly. A *Sunday Times* poll placed M.P.s eighth on an index of trustworthiness – doctors, judges, lawyers, civil servants, Cabinet ministers, union leaders and even local legislators are rated higher than M.P.s, in that order. The M.P.s have one consolation. The integrity of journalists is as suspect as their own.

In the end, though, it is not public cynicism towards M.P.s which has undermined Parliament, but a kind of mindless romanticism amongst its members. The belief in the protective powers of oratory is one manifestation of this; another even more seductive influence is the concept of sovereignty. Powell, for example, talks of 'the sheer pride in being a member of this sovereign assembly'. The word 'sovereign' is a key to the emotional defence-mechanism of True Brit, suggesting something that is threatened by nasty Europeans and all alien beings. Britain's entry into Europe has served to revive all the phobias that can be stirred in the British breast at the drop of the word 'sovereignty', which, like the English Constitution, is more spiritual than substantial. Sovereignty is like virginity: you're never the same without it. Just say the word to John Bull and he snarls with vigilant patriotism.

Parliament is the latest British institution to complete the transition from a working instrument into a ritualistic myth; the first to do so was the monarchy. But whereas Parliament is pointless without its power, the monarchy has, in its impotence, gained a role.

The key to the importance of the monarchy as an institution is its placebo effect. It works because it has no power. It has no power because it is above power. If the ultimate allegiance of the people were to anything less mythical – to a general, a politician, even (like the French) a banker – the current morbidity would make the head of state very insecure. Disenchanted generals in Britain cannot enforce their views with a *coup d'état* because it is not the Prime Minister they would have to depose, but the Crown. That is unthinkable. This would also be proof against cabals of businessmen.

Even when a political decision divides the country on issues of patriotism, as it did with the unilateral declaration of independence by the white supremacists of Rhodesia, the Queen manages to appear neutral and it is impossible to guess where her sympathies lie. The Rhodesians still swear allegiance to the throne, believing themselves to be more British than the British. At the same time they are stigmatized as rebels against the Crown. No contradiction seems apparent to them. In the same way, the erosion of 'sovereignty' required by joining the Common Market needed the formality of Royal assent, and nobody thought to ask whether the Queen actually liked being diminished in this way.

The fiction that the Queen plays an assenting and advising role in government is religiously sustained by politicians. At their weekly audience with the Queen, Prime Ministers are now allowed to sit, rather than stand. This concession literally swept Harold Macmillan off his feet. Asserting that the influence of the monarch has actually increased, he recalls in *Pointing the Way*, the fourth volume of his memoirs:

> The Queen has a right as well as a duty to be fully informed of all the affairs not only of the United Kingdom but also of all the countries of the Commonwealth, as well as of foreign countries. This duty was always conscientiously performed. All Cabinet papers, all departmental papers, all foreign telegrams are sent to her, and carefully studied by her. All the Cabinet's decisions which, under the Cabinet Secretarial system are rapidly and accurately circulated, are available to her immediately ... the Queen has the absolute right to know, to criticize, to advise.

This picture of Royal dedication to affairs of state is hard to swallow. All Cabinet ministers complain that they can't get through their own papers. The prospect of digesting

this cataract of paper every day would be daunting for anyone with nothing else to do, and nobody imagines that the
Queen is that dedicated. The most assiduously studied
paper in Buckingham Palace is probably *Sporting Life*, for
its extensive coverage of horse-racing. The monarchy
doesn't need propping up or being made to look powerful
by fawning politicians.

It was a happy accident that gave the country a queen
when it did. A king would not have been right; the mood
would not have favoured him. A patriarch without an
empire would have been too out of place, too much the last
of the Romanovs, too much a reminder of what was gone, too
clearly redundant.

But a queen, especially one capable of turning from a
fairy princess into a homely matron, offers succour to the
depleted ego. As the country turns in on itself it needs her
maternal embrace. There is no other bosom to cry onto.
This is not the brave 'Second Elizabethan Age' proclaimed
at her Coronation, but a maudlin time that this woman suits
well. As long as she remains, the Crown will seem relevant.
When she goes, it may not be so secure.

The Court of Elizabeth II is a shrewdly stage-managed
fantasy, part de Mille, part Ruritanian, part Noël Coward,
part P. G. Wodehouse. Over the years the monarchy has
learned to adapt, though often more in appearance than in
fact. The Royal Family has been de-formalized but not de-
mystified. Its duties have been made to look onerous while
its comforts have remained lavish. It has kept its riches but
claimed penury. It has appeared united, the exemplary
nuclear family, while riven with temperament. The slight-
est suggestion that the Queen dozes on the job arouses
hysterical counter-claims. An ad-man never worked harder
for a detergent account. When the Queen asked Parliament for more money, her advisers produced an absurd list
of her arduous duties. She could never take 'a complete
holiday' (she spends a third of every year in her rural
houses). Even her acknowledged recreations are portrayed

as dutiful: 'The Queen and the Royal Family are well known as supporters of sport and athletics.' The domestic touch is not neglected: 'As well as carrying the exceptional burdens of Sovereignty, the Queen carries also those common to all wives and mothers.' And, leaving nothing to chance: 'The Queen is an owner-breeder of thoroughbred race horses and her successes on the turf give pleasure to a large section of the public who are interested in breeding and racing.'

Since the Queen's accession, the cost of running the show has gone from £1·2m. to £4·7m. a year, a rise of 280 per cent. While the Queen herself needn't have resorted to a contrived defence of her way of life, the comforts of her relatives are a more vulnerable point. Her mother's household includes two peers, seven army officers, a Mistress of the Robes, two Ladies of the Bedchamber, three Extra Ladies of the Bedchamber, four Women of the Bedchamber and six Extra Women of the Bedchamber.

The Queen's sister, Princess Margaret, is probably the least popular of the whole family. She has been called 'this expensive kept woman' by Willie Hamilton, M.P., the vigorous Republican. Her house has cost the taxpayer £80,000 so far, and she gets £35,000 a year tax-free. But it is not so much these expenses that displease the public as her glowering demeanour and increasingly plain appearance. As one sister has become mature and steady as the monarch, the other seems to have gone sour and irascible. Something of the same mood afflicts Lord Snowdon. Life in the glass cage has not worked out too well for him.

But the most volatile temperament in the Royal Family is Prince Philip's. For a man who was fairly hard up when he married into the family and who now gets £65,000 a year from the public coffers, as well as a hefty subsidy from his wife, Philip seems singularly impatient with his patrons. He leads the life of a Royal James Bond, switching from helicopter to private plane to racing yacht to fast car to royal yacht as he swings annually around the world, usually managing to be in agreeable corners of the South Pacific and other temperate zones when the British winter is at its worst. In 1971, for example, he was able to visit on his own (among other places) Canada, Grand Bahama, the Galapagos Islands, Fiji, New Guinea, Australia, Bahrain, Budapest, and Iran. The Royal yacht *Britannia*, on which his three-month winter cruise took place, costs £1m. a year to run.

All this activity is presented as a selfless endurance test carried out in the public interest. Lord Cobbold, the Lord Chamberlain, is so anxious to uphold the idea that Philip has sacrificed all for the Crown that he has actually said: 'It seems only reasonable to me that in the case of someone doing a full-time job and precluded from earning the high salary which he would undoubtedly command in the outside world there should be a considerable element of real remuneration.' The only 'outside job' which could match Philip's income and life-style is held down by Aristotle Onassis, and the two do, at least, have a bond of birth.

In the early 1940s George VI and his Queen had 'arranged' the courtship of their daughter Elizabeth and Prince Philip Mountbatten. Snobs in London society disapproved. They thought the couple were too interrelated. The Mountbattens' most Anglicized representative was the young Elizabeth's uncle, Lord Louis. The Mountbatten blood mingled the Royal lines of Denmark, Germany and Greece, but many monarchies were crumbling. Philip's father Prince Andrew was content to play out the role of the philandering Ruritanian on the Riviera, while Philip was being 'blooded' in battle with the Royal Navy, under the tutelage of Lord Louis. The Battle of the Mediterranean, tough as it turned out to be, must have been preferable to an aimless life amongst the discards of the old thrones (although Philip's professional dedication to the Navy went with a touch of his father's roving eye). His emergence in Westminster Abbey in 1947 as the handsome fairy prince slowed him down a bit, but the frequent cracking of his cool since then is an obvious sign of biting at the bridle.

All the same, the public is very forgiving. Philip makes sober matrons swoon, and even Labour Prime Ministers have been known to genuflect. He shrewdly knows how much rope is available to him, and he uses all of it. The principal victims of his public outbursts are well chosen: journalists. It is a target that the British would choose themselves. So that when, as he has, Philip throws nuts at both the Barbary apes and reporters in Gibraltar, or tells photographers in Jamaica that they are 'bloody clots', or says to another photographer in Beirut 'stuff that camera up your arse', he is sure that these trained masochists will both report his action and turn the other cheek. There is something cocky in the Prince that the British would like to see in other public figures.

His actual contribution to society is negligible. He sponsors Teutonic-style expeditions for young men who fancy the rugged life; he promotes the preservation of wild life while his daughter rides with impunity with the foxhunters; he gives occasional jingoistic speeches exhorting exporters to bigger deals; he endorses the diplomatic relationship with fascist states like Portugal. There is not really a job there, but his public relations are, usually by his own devising, expertly managed. And that is, after all, what keeps the fantasy of monarchy viable.

Philip's short fuse has been inherited most noticeably by his daughter. The constraints on the life of a young Princess are not what they were when Princess Margaret was sternly discouraged by the Archbishop of Canterbury from marrying Peter Townsend, the rakish Battle of Britain hero. But for a girl with the drives of Anne they are still enough to provoke frequent minor rebellions. She once cut a swathe through the socially approved but effete young stags of London. As well as being headstrong like her father, Anne has contracted her mother's horse mania. The listless and decorative life which might otherwise have been her lot has been replaced by dedication to the saddle. This, in turn, diverted her from the playgrounds of the *Almanach de Gotha* into the arms of the British squirearchy, a close-knit society where the horse is god.

It is also the breeding ground of another kind of thorough-bred, the kind of young man who once went off with the Hussars to the Peninsular war. He is a fusion of sportsman and soldier. It is not a world where brains count for much. Physical courage is at a premium. When Anne met her Dragoon it was soon clear who was the stronger of the two personalities. Mark Phillips was awed by Anne as both horsewoman and companion. As a husband he is helped by the esoteric bond of equestrians; both he and Anne could ride horses before they could walk. But he's going to find his wife as hot-blooded as any young colt. She is extremely competitive and strong-willed, and the marriage is going to be more public and more eventful than any in the Royal Family since Wallis Simpson found her King.

The wedding of Anne and Mark Phillips obliged the national psychology. Another pageant in Westminster Abbey, an orgy of ritualistic sentiment, was the kind of tonic True Brit sorely needed. In this sense the Royal Family is an impeccably trained branch of show-business. They know just how to open the withering glands of national pride, to conjure the last juices from the most cynical breast. It is the one thing they do really well, and for which there is no substitute. Coming at a time of increasing disenchantment with the Common Market, the wedding seemed also to be an aggressive reassertion of all the mythical Anglo-Saxon qualities, an answer to the bland and anonymous sovereignty of the bureaucrat.

But it was really too late. Brussels is already closer than Westminster Abbey. The old monarchs might spin in their tombs, but the millennium is complete.

Perhaps Prince Charles senses his own impending re-dundancy. By the time he becomes King the country will be unrecognizable. His subjects will be governed by Euro-pean laws. His Parliament, already enfeebled, will be no better than a rubber stamp. His country will be paved over and cemented to Europe by the needs of the corporate state, like a none-too-efficient manufacturing subsidiary. With these imperatives the monarchy will lose credence. Minds that care little for palaces and castles are going to be increasingly impatient to find them still occupied. The Royal Family will become the reproving ghosts of a lost identity.

For the moment, the Queen puts a stoic face on things. She is not shrewish, she is not imperious (once the only *persona* for a monarch), she is not neglectful, and she is not in any way ridiculous. She seems to want to be accepted as more real, but how real can a Queen be? She has been led into little public-relations tricks like 'walkabouts', to suggest a more touchable monarch. But these produce brief and often awkward chats with the plebs and change nothing. The Queen obviously wishes that they were convincing, but the glass cage filters out too much reality. It is unnatural for her to be natural.

In its present state the monarchy is relatively harmless – relative, that is, to the corrupting political monarchies of the American and French Presidencies. The Queen is at least above all that, and although she stays above it by being in the clouds it is not bad for people to be able to look up occasionally. It takes their eyes and their minds off the mess below.

The euphoric effect of the monarchy is not lost on the British Press. A royal wedding can wipe all news, especially bad news, off not only the front page but virtually off every page. Twenty-four hours after the nation had stopped to watch Anne take her Mark, the London *Times* could still accord this event more space than the worst economic emergency since the war. The complicity of the British Press in sustaining the Pollyanna tendency of True Brit is manifest.

A country that is constantly taken by surprise as it falls apart is being kept in the dark by the people who are supposed to be shining the light. Surprise is, after all, the child of ignorance. The British don't know why things are so bad for them because they aren't being told. One reason why they're not being told is that the Press is dilatory. Another reason is that the architects of the disaster enjoy the most effective security blanket in any supposedly democratic system.

Richard Crossman, a former Leader of the House of Commons and a Constitutionalist, holds that British government is 'the biggest coverer-up that's ever been'. He points out that nearly twenty years after the Suez imbroglio many of the details of the collusion between British and French governments are still safely locked away. There was a massive deception of Parliament, but no inquiry.

In a society like America, bruised into cynicism by successive scandals in the highest places, it is still possible to find the system redeeming because of the visibility of its corruption and the tradition of exposing it. Britain prefers the pretence that the privacy of power is essential to maintain its integrity, a reversion of logic that is defended assiduously. The parliamentary system assumes that accountability rests with ministers because they hold the power. Discounting the sham of parliamentary procedure from this assumption, it would still be meaningless because the real power that needs to be held accountable is not there anyway.

It is no coincidence that the most oppressive part of institutionalized secrecy in Britain dates from the inchoate phase of the central bureaucracy. In the course of one sleepy afternoon in the late summer of 1911 the House of Commons passed the Official Secrets Act with only the most casual scrutiny and debate. It was an astute piece of timing by the Executive. There was a widespread paranoia about German spies, and the new legislation seemed to be an essential strengthening of national security. But this was deceptive. Although the first section of the Act was indeed aimed at espionage, the second part gave the bureaucrats an unprecedented degree of confidentiality, at the time when their power to intervene in the life of the country was to steadily escalate.

The combining of the two motives in one Act judged the British mood expertly. An Act giving civil servants immunity to inconvenient surveillance would, on its own, have been too conspicuous. But put alongside the preservation of national security in the face of the dreadful Huns it became tangled in patriotism. The impression was easily created that to challenge the Official Secrets Act was against the national interest – more than insolence, it was treachery. This deception held good for more than sixty years. Under its cover the Custodians have not only consolidated their hold; they have assumed a perpetual right to subversive activity.

Some of the things that the British are not allowed to know about those who rule them show how great is the arrogant self-assurance allowed by tradition. They also show the difference between apparent and real power. At the centre of government the decision-making rests not so much with ministers as with sixteen Cabinet committees. Neither the names nor the composition of these committees are disclosed. The Cabinet Office's explanation in its evidence to the Franks Committee on the Official Secrets Act, was:

> The decisions of these committees, as indeed the decisions of individual Ministers, are as much decisions of the Government as are decisions of the Cabinet itself. No Government, therefore, discloses the list of their committees, their membership or scope, for to do so would be liable to impair collective responsibility as well as detract from the individual responsibility of Ministers.

A more explicit denial of the principle of accountability could hardly be imagined. In effect this is saying that neither 'collective' nor individual decisions can be traceable. From this it follows that policies and decisions should be seen as completely impersonal, conceived in a vacuum. Business executives would find this idea congenial. On these principles there is no way of either Parliament or the public knowing on what grounds a crucial decision has been taken, or of understanding its motivation or judging its quality. The results are not exactly reassuring. For example, one of the secret committees is the Regional Policy and Environmental Committee, controlling projects involving about £20,000 million of public money. It is the clearing house for airports, motorways and edifices of all kinds.

It is in work of this kind that secrecy takes on the justification of 'expertise'. Planners develop a kind of 'project maternalism'; their babies are so long in gestation that any challenge to their conception provokes an intense and jealous protectiveness. Their objective is to conceal their real intentions until they are beyond recall. And they do it with impunity. A leak of plans to curtail the British Rail network was enough to send Scotland Yard's Special Branch interrogating reporters and editors, searching their files and hounding them at their homes. This was the mechanism of the police state in action, carried out under the pretext of the Official Secrets Act.

But the Act was challenged, and it did seem possible that it had fatally overreached itself. *The Sunday Telegraph* published a confidential British military report on Nigeria. Compared to the Pentagon Papers it was a trifle, but in Westminster the Wilson government's reaction was apoplectic. After a controversial trial, Mr Justice Caulfield threw out the government's case and said the Official Secrets Act should be 'pensioned off'. Some time later he explained that what really worried him was the way the Act could be 'viciously or capriciously used by an embarrassed Executive'. When a liberal judge talks like this, suspicion of the Executive can't be lightly dismissed as radical paranoia.

Certainly, the Custodians are agile in dealing with threats to their security. They proposed an Information Act to replace the Secrets Act. The use of a positive word like 'information' ought to have been a warning; language was being manipulated. This new device was outlined to the

House of Commons under circumstances strangely similar to the somnolent debate of 1911: it was a Friday in summer and many M.P.s had already left town; the Chamber was sparsely attended. At first the new Act was taken at face value, as a reform. Then it became clear, when the official ambiguities were deciphered, that the real purpose was to shroud government in even greater secrecy. The pivotal Cabinet committees would remain invisible, and all decision-making would stay anonymous. There was no intention of following the lead of the American Freedom of Information Act, which critics had called for. In America the onus is on the government to justify a refusal to disclose material; in Britain any civil servant disclosing information faces criminal charges (in Sweden he faces charges if he does not). But the British system goes well beyond the concealment of contemporary decision-making. All government papers are kept from public scrutiny for thirty years; some, defined as 'highly sensitive', are official secrets for 100 years.

By parliamentary convention, a government can make any subject taboo simply by persistently refusing to answer questions about it. The list of such subjects now includes affairs as grave as 'the day to day matters' of the White Fish Authority, forecasts of changes in food prices, the trade statistics for Scotland, discipline in schools, and the operation of ferry services. More significantly, it also includes details of arms sales (Britain is a major clandestine gun-runner), accident rates of aircraft, telephone taps, the reasons for allowing a merger, and details of sterling balances. The priorities between the public interest and private government are clear.

Where, in the face of all this suppression, are the scavengers of the Press?

British newspapers include some of the most salacious and trivial in the world. Like the country itself, the newspapers adhere to class allegiances. You are what you read. At the top you read *The Times*, or, if you claim a social conscience, *The Guardian*. The *bourgeoisie* read *The Daily Telegraph*, which, like its readers, practises the native hypocrisies by concealing under a grey exterior an alert eye for fruity courtroom details. The plebs take either the *Daily Mirror*, now getting a little hard in the arteries, or the *Sun*, the impudent and appalling creation of the Australian interloper Rupert Murdoch. Drifting in the middle, with the confusions of the lower middle class, are the *Daily Mail* and the *Daily Express*. The *Express* is the most blatantly racist paper in Britain, and stands to the last with the white supremacists of Rhodesia. The only consistently aggressive and serious journalism comes on Sunday, in *The Observer*, *The Sunday Times*, and, occasionally, *The Sunday Telegraph*. To balance this, Sunday also produces the *News of the World*, known to its 16 million readers as the 'Screws of the World'. Its view of the world is exclusively carnal; this was the paper that performed the public service of photographing Lord Lambton with his pants down (but not printing the result). It was also the paper that disinterred Christine Keeler's memoirs. Rupert Murdoch, who also owns the *News of the World*, has shown a fine instinct for winning readers and losing influence.

The combined artillery of the Press (to use Jefferson's phrase) produces not so much a bang as a whimper. It is no match for clandestine government. Where vigilance matters most, British editors are blind. Their reporters are still where the power is supposed to be, in Westminster, rather than where it is, in Whitehall. It is only a couple of blocks away, but it could be a thousand miles. Not one London paper has a reporter assigned to Whitehall. The understanding of central government gets scant regard.

The lapdogs of the Westminster lobby don't always earn the affection they crave. Harold Wilson, one of the most skilful manipulators of the Press, can still be as paranoid as Richard Nixon, suspecting a plot under or between every line. Talking about himself in the third person, Wilson says: 'The virulence with which the Labour leader is pursued by the Conservative Press is out of all proportion to that against the Conservative leader.' But at least Wilson's persecution mania is out in the open. On the left wing of his party there are more sinister ideas and men, like Anthony Wedgwood Benn, who has called on the labour unions within newspapers 'to see that what is said about us is true.' Even without his encouragement, unions often threaten to shut down a paper unless it holds its tongue about their own activities. Industrial sabotage on the presses is frequent, but unreported.

The Press's endemic weakness is that it reflects the traditional deference of the British towards their institutions, and their awe of authority. Newspapers will readily do what they have been convinced is patriotic, even if it means keeping quiet. Sir Gordon Newton, former editor of the *Financial Times*, for example, confessed to the Franks Committee that for two years he kept out of the paper any story hinting that sterling might be devalued, which it subsequently was. He now says he would never do it again, but the fact that an influential specialist paper can deliberately suppress bad news gives some measure of British editorial spunk. Jingoism and the pursuit of True Brit are stronger motives than scepticism. It is a case of the blind leading the blind.

7 *The law by which all law is judged:*
The lion and the flea, and other stories

English law is the sacred core of True Brit. Of all those
parts of the British idea which have been dispersed about
the world, the common law of the English is still the most
revered. Its hold now has something of the mystique of the
holy scriptures. Senator Sam Ervin, explaining the genius
of the men who created the American Constitution,
expresses the power of the idea: 'So they went through all
the great documents of the English law, from the Magna
Carta on down, and whatever they found there they in-
corporated in the Constitution, to preserve the liberties of
the people.'

This kind of talk is resonant with the romanticism of
Anglophilia. The idea has somehow transcended the
pragmatism of history, as a tablet ennobles a chisel. Looking at the American reverence for English law, the British
ought to feel as the Greeks now do towards democracy:
translations wear better than the originals. In the hands of
the Custodians English law is a sorry mess. In Whitehall
the infection of True Brit is necessarily covert; in the courts
it surfaces in the more conspicuous role of an enforcement
agency. If it rests on anything, English law rests on the concept of dispassionate justice, detached from and above the
petty allegiances of men and self-serving motives. And yet,
on their recent form, the courts have been fierce in defence
of the powerful and dilatory in defence of the weak. Take,
for a start, the case of the thalidomide children.

Whisky advertisements like to give the impression of a
cottage industry, a part-mystical process in which the rare
waters of Highland streams are transformed into a golden

ambrosia by a race of men with canny noses. Like most businesses which have seen a local demand turn into an international fashion, whisky distillers trade on their tradition long after the realities of mass production have made the original plant a museum piece.

There still seems to be a healthy diversity of choice in the whisky market: among the brands lining liquor-store shelves, five of the most ubiquitous are Johnnie Walker, Haig, Dewar's, Black and White, and White Horse. In fact, all of these are produced by the same company. So are Vat 69, King George IV, and the rarer *de luxe* whiskies like the Antiquary, Crawford's, and Talisker. So are Gordon's, the world's largest-selling gin, Booth's gin, High & Dry gin, Cossack vodka, and the staple of colonial sundowners, Pimm's Cups. The happy provider of all this inner warmth is the Distillers Company of Edinburgh and Glasgow.

The Distillers Company is the corporate extension of the Scottish character. It is wealthy, secretive, prudent in its accounting, and most of its executives share a passion for the sport that the Scots invented, golf. But the company has more than traditional reasons for keeping a low profile. With 60 per cent of the world market for Scotch whisky and a stranglehold on the British liquor market it is anxious not to attract the attentions of anti-monopolists. Its pre-tax profit in 1973 was more than £70m.

In 1961 several British medical journals carried advertisements for a drug called Distaval which said: 'Distaval [thalidomide] can be given with complete safety to pregnant women and nursing mothers without adverse effect on mother and child.' The makers of Distaval were a Distillers' subsidiary, Distillers (Biochemicals) Ltd, who manufactured it under licence from Chemie Grunenthal, a German company. Less than a month after the Distaval advertisements ran in Britain the drug was withdrawn. A causal relationship had been established between thalidomide and deformities in children whose mothers had taken the drug during pregnancy.

In Britain there were 400 families faced with the night-mare of raising children lacking some or all of their limbs, and with other cruel mutations. In November 1962 the first writ alleging negligence by the Distillers Company was served by the father of a child born without arms. Ten years later, abstruse legal arguments – seemingly remote from the human tragedy they concerned – were still being rehearsed in the British courts. The law proved singularly confused and unrewarding for the parents. And the Distillers Company had been no more compassionate than the courts.

To have proved the drug manufacturers negligent in law would have been more straightforward if injury had been caused after birth. The drug had done its damage at a point when English law did not recognize the victim as a living soul. Under American law there is a precedent covering the foetus; there is none in England. Because the foetus issue was 'unsolved' in English law, the litigation bogged down on the issue of negligence. It was a formula for the kind of elegant procrastination which sends lawyers' fees on a spree, like an unstoppable taxi-meter. There were 30,000 docu-ments from the Distillers' files to be gone through. Some parents were advised that they had no case and could not sue; others thought it unnecessary to sue because Distillers would provide for them; many did not even know that their children were deformed by thalidomide because they didn't know they had taken the drug.

The mark on the children was obvious enough, but the burden on the parents became acute. Financial strains reduced some families to penury; psychological stress shattered previously ordered lives.

The first settlement by Distillers did not reach court until 1968. Only fifty-eight of the children were involved. Their parents had been persuaded that to prove 'a duty of care to a foetus', in the detached language of the lawyers, could not be guaranteed. Settlement was devised accord-ing to abject conditions. The counsel for the parents said he would accept 40 per cent of whatever 'normal liability for injury' was judged to be by the court. English law is so deficient in assessing damages for personal injury that the Law Commission, responsible for reform, says it lacks 'any mathematical, actuarial, statistical or other scientific basis'. Not to mention something as abstract as compassion. The judge thought Distillers were very generous in their approach and said it would be 'folly to refuse such an offer'. The average sum per child worked out at £14,000. On an actuarial basis it would have been about £45,000–£50,000 per child.

To pacify the parents of another 374 victims, Distillers proposed a charitable trust fund worth £3·25m. To each child this was worth £7,500, just over half the previous settlement. The parents were told by the lawyers that this compared 'very favourably' with settlements in other countries. In Sweden similar awards were worth about £50,000 per child, and in the U.S.A. between £100,000 and £150,000.

The steel in the eye of Distillers began to show. The trust fund would be available only if *all* the parents agreed to it. When five held out, *their own lawyers* pressed them to settle, threatened that legal aid would be withdrawn, and made other minatory noises. They even tried to establish that the defiant parents were unacceptable as representatives of their own children's interests, and to put their case in the hands of the Official Solicitor, who would presumably have joined the more compliant parents. When this case came to court the whole Distillers' case slowly began to unravel.

The Appeal Court ruled for the resisting parents. But before this the newspapers had begun to wake up to what was going on. 'SCANDALOUS!' declared the *Daily Mail*. The day after the paper got a letter from Kimber, Bull, the company of lawyers acting for the parents. The paper, said the lawyers, had committed a 'clear contempt of court'. The three words 'contempt of court' have for years constituted the biggest booby-trap in the path of campaigning editors, more intimidating than even the punitive libel laws. No comment was permissible on cases before the courts; any coverage at all if proceedings were 'contemplated' was similarly *sub judice*. This was really an ingenious trap, since the only people to judge if a court case was imminent were the shadowy and often dilatory official prosecutors. If they said a case was 'contemplated', nobody could prove otherwise. The letter from Kimber, Bull precipitated exactly the kind of situation where the law seemed at its worst.

It was technically true that the parents and the Distillers were involved in litigation, but the wrangling had gone on for so long – for most of the time out of court – that it could almost have been regarded as dormant. The details were so complex, and the lawyers so stricken with constipation that there was little, if any, prospect of a case being brought to trial. In the event the *Daily Mail* decided to call the bluff, and ran a second story. What happened then involves a figure at the centre of English law, and its most questionable aspects. The Attorney-General intervened.

Although this was a civil, not a criminal action, and although no court was in session, the Attorney-General *appeared on behalf of Distillers*. He warned that a formal complaint had been made of contempt of court – but it had been made by Kimber, Bull, who were acting on behalf of the parents, not the drug company! The *Daily Mail* was stopped in its tracks.

The office of the Attorney-General originated in the thirteenth century, its function to preserve the royal interests in court. Today he is one of the three 'Law officers of the Crown'. The other two are the Solicitor-General and, the most senior of the trio, the Lord Chancellor. They are political appointees and members of the government. The tradition is that Attorneys-General plead 'no political motive', even in cases where a political motive would have seemed reasonable and rational – in, for example, the leakage of secrets. To regard their role as anything but ambivalent requires generous credulity.

Although this time Sir Peter Rawlinson, Edward Heath's Attorney-General, had gagged the press, their timidity was not to last. For several years the assiduous investigating team of *The Sunday Times* had been building up a file on Distillers and thalidomide. Late in 1972 they ran a three-page introduction to what they promised would be a definitive account of the matter. With only this trailer to go on, the Attorney-General materialized again, this time asking for an injunction – on behalf of Distillers – to restrain publication of the second article. The paper allowed him to read the second article in draft and he decided that it would exert 'undue pressure' on Distillers. Bearing in mind the harrowing and relentless pressure applied by the company on the parents to capitulate to its settlement offer, the right response would have been a hollow laugh.

But the judges of the High Court were more sombre. They managed to disinter a precedent from 1742 to help establish that: 'The test of contempt is whether the words complained of create a serious risk that the course of justice may be interfered with.' The writs in the thalidomide case had been issued *four years* earlier; the prospect of bringing them to court was not taken seriously. The preservation of the dignity and processes of the law was, apparently, more important than either the public interest or the children's.

The Attorney-General said his duty was 'to mind generally the public interest, the fair administration of justice and the interests of the court.' The High Court decided that the *Sunday Times* story should be suppressed. But the Appeal Court did not agree. The case developed into a contest of learned nabobs.

In the Appeal Court Lord Denning pointed out that the proposed Distillers Trust Fund represented little more than 1 per cent of the profits of Distillers in the ten years since the tragedy. He found the Attorney-General's intervention strange, and he was critical of the lawyers: 'these actions have gone soundly to sleep ... no one has awakened them.

I think I can see why.' But the Attorney-General was obdurate. When the Appeal Court ruled in favour of *The Sunday Times*, he went to the court of last resort, the House of Lords. After painfully slow deliberation, they supported the gag. But by that time the law's impotence was overtaken by events.

Throughout the whole saga the taciturn chairman of Distillers, Sir Alex McDonald, had avoided any public appearances or pronouncements. Distillers had long since sold its drugs business to Eli Lilly, the American firm. The company had, in any case, prudently taken out insurance against claims from the public (one of the members of the Lloyd's syndicate concerned was Sir Keith Joseph, later Edward Heath's Minister of Health; Patrick Jenkin, another Heath minister, had been an employee of Distillers).

Distillers was parsimonious in its own business. Apart from the directors, only one out of its 19,000 employees earned more than a four-figure salary. The board was a mixture of canny accountants like McDonald, liquor technicians, and a few quasi-aristocratic whisky family heirs. There was also Henry Evelyn Alexander Dewar, third baron Forteviot, and the largest personal shareholder. The kilted Lord Forteviot lives in a castle surrounded by 15,000 acres of park. The estate is intersected by public roads, but the staff cut down bushes growing along the verge to discourage passing drivers from stopping to pick blackberries.

Distillers' public demeanour was similar. Uproar over thalidomide in Parliament and the Press seemed to the men in Scotland typical of hysteria in London, that flashy and dangerous city. In Edinburgh, McDonald, who looks like a bulkier version of Khruschev, lives a simple social life. No Edinburgh magnate, so long as he stays there, needs to worry much about critical scrutiny by the Scottish news-papers – a servile and parochial bunch. And the Distillers' shareholders, who got more than £24m. out of the company in 1972, were happy. But none the less it was through some of its shareholders that Distillers was finally led to its conscience.

The company is attractive to institutional investors wanting consistent earnings and guaranteed growth. Two insurance companies, the Prudential and the Britannic, have between them nearly 4 per cent of Distillers' shares – a large enough portion to be influential because of the dispersion of most holdings. Financial leverage is one thing, but moral influence has not been regarded as a congenital characteristic of large financial institutions. However, some of the shrewder lobbyists on behalf of the thalidomide parents, enraged by the reticence of Sir Alex McDonald and his fellow directors, sought out these institutional shareholders. They were helped by some discreet political pressure. Distillers finally coughed up a new settlement worth seven times the original trust fund, involving £20m. to be paid in instalments over ten years, averaging about £55,000 for each child.

Ten years of legal shadow-boxing had been fruitless; six months of a Press campaign, although legally emasculated, had extracted the appropriate social response. A new sanction had been used against corporate intransigence, the leverage of the institutional shareholder. The clown of the story, if not the villain, was the law.

If corporate morality produced black comedy in the courts, the quagmire of sexual morality has been an equally unhappy test of True Brit. In 1960 the British were finally allowed to read *Lady Chatterley's Lover* in its uncensored form, thirty-two years after it was written by Lawrence. But the *Lady Chatterley* trial turned out to be a false dawn for literary and sexual liberty. It is a basic tenet of True Brit that sex is too dangerous to be enjoyed by peasants: 'Is it the kind of book you would want your servants to read?' had been the rubric of the Crown's case against the publishers of *Lady Chatterley*. The gyrations of the higher courts as they chase the Rampant Penis are inelegant, contradictory, and intemperate. There was, for example, the *Oz* case.

It was the longest obscenity trial in English history. *Oz* was a garish, semi-literate magazine created by Richard Neville, an Australian. There was a gleam in Neville's eye suggesting that he wanted an Aussie's revenge on the Pommies, and planned to lure the courts into action which would end in their being ridiculed. If so, it worked.

The trial of *Oz*, for an issue aimed at children, found in Judge Argyle the kind of stern Victorian hand that the Puritans yearned for. Displaying contempt for 'expert' witnesses called by the defence, Argyle imposed two prison sentences, stiff fines, and – a final touch of the old colonialism – recommended that Neville should be deported, like the convicts who were the original involuntary settlers of British Australia.

These draconian penalties were removed by the judges of the Appeal Court. But their lordships then became muddled over the meanings of 'indecent', 'obscene', 'lewd', 'filthy' and 'repulsive'. In the confusion, they put new constraints on publishers. They ruled that although a book could be judged as a whole, a newspaper or magazine could be offensive if any single article, illustration or cartoon were ruled to be capable of 'depraving or corrupting'. The Appeal Court also disqualified the testimony of expert witnesses, and gave its warning that prison sentences could be expected in future cases. Neville's flea had certainly aroused the lion, probably by biting its balls.

The *Oz* trial (in 1971) was an extreme case of True Brit overreaching itself. Some judges are much shrewder in dealing with provocation. In the Angry Brigade trial (in 1972), the longest and most expensive in British legal history, Mr Justice James de-fused what the radical left had expected to be a show political trial. He allowed the defence to reject thirty-nine jurors on political grounds; he allowed three of the accused to conduct their own defence; and he allowed great latitude in defence submissions, particularly challenges to police evidence. Four of the 'Stoke Newington Eight' were jailed for ten years, the other four acquitted for reasons which implied that the jury believed the police had planted evidence. The sentences were not light, but Chris Bott, one of those who was acquitted admitted afterwards:

> It was a victory for the judge, and for the tactics he adopted. He ran it very intelligently indeed. We could win against the prosecution, but we couldn't win against him, because he refused to take a class position. He insisted on remaining impartial, interpreting only the law and directing the jury to do the same.

Many of the Custodians might well have favoured making an example of the Eight. Instead the Bench kept its cool. There were no martyrs. But the police were not happy. They complained that the law was weighted too far in favour of the defence and too little in favour of the prosecution. It is this view which is causing the most serious lesion in the agencies of the law. It is an argument that shows the most repressive temper of the Custodians, and it is so fundamental to the image of English law that it has aroused concern outside the country. Doctor Manfred Simon, formerly of the Court of Appeal of Paris, became so concerned by what was being said that he wrote to *The Times* in October 1972 and said: 'Any changes which would endanger the proper protection given by the English system to the accused are a matter of general, not merely English concern.'

The rights of a suspect under English law are already inferior to those in America. Interrogation inside police stations takes place without a lawyer or witnesses. The suspect can be detained for long periods without access to his lawyer and without any charges being brought (even Spain is more liberal in this respect). But this was not enough for the committee set up under Lord Justice Edmund Davies to review criminal-law procedures.

The Davies committee wanted to erode the suspect's rights even more. It recommended (in its report published in 1972) the virtual abolition of the 'right to silence' both under police interrogation and during trial; much wider admission of hearsay evidence; and the increased admissibility of evidence of any previous record on the accused. The police were delighted. Jurists were stunned. The changes would, said Dr Simon, 'introduce into English law certain features of the so-called inquisitorial procedure, as applied in France, without establishing at the same time safeguards comparable to those, imperfect as they may be, which have been inserted into French legislation with a view to protecting the accused.'

Even more alarming to this foreign observer was that the changes suggested 'the first timid attempt to dismantle the venerable fortress built by many generations of British lawyers to protect the innocent – a sad illustration of the insidious process whereby standards of even the most civilized countries can, under modern pressures, subtly but irresistibly be eroded'.

Trial lawyers who appear for both the defence and prosecution refute the police case that things are loaded against them. Aware also of the increasingly dubious methods of the police, these lawyers, representing the Bar Council, rejected the Davies committee's ideas and said (in 1972): 'We would have expected the maintenance of safeguards for the individual against oppression or malicious or vindictive prosecution to have been at the very centre of an inquiry ... and this is the more so when public confidence in the police in some parts of the country is in question.' They want to move towards the American system, and as a further safeguard they want any statement made after the police have refused access to a lawyer to be declared inadmissible. But the really significant thing about the response of the barristers is that they have, virtually *en masse*, emerged as the real libertarians, between a reactionary judiciary on the one hand and the police hard-liners on the other. The fissure is serious. It reveals not only a professional dispute but a political polarity. Lawyers do not lightly talk of 'malicious or vindictive prosecution.' If the criminal law is vulnerable to naked political pressures, the outcome could be catastrophic.

The political pressures have, if anything, been aggravated by an increasingly political instinct in the police hierarchy. At one time, whatever the sentiments of the top policemen they were not inclined towards the subtleties of political lobbying. As late as 1971 the Association of Chief Police Officers submitted a memorandum to the Franks Committee recommending the retention of the whole of the Official Secrets Act in such unambiguous terms ('journalists are prone to put forward a view that publication of official matters is in the public interest') that it was counterproductive. But the police have now gained a leader who is much more plausible.

Sir Robert Mark, the Commissioner of the Metropolitan Police, has shown skilled political footwork throughout his rapid rise to the top. Mark has been shrewd enough to secure his lines of communication with the Home Office, and the degree to which he is now sanctioned as the social philosopher of the 'law and order' lobby was shown by his remarkable 1973 Dimbleby Lecture on B.B.C. television. Like the studio audience, *The Times* was ready to rhapsodize over this performance as 'excellent and lucid'. But a more considered analysis of what he said, and the way he said it, is less reassuring.

Mark adopted the didactic simplicity of a policeman explaining the highway code to a school, and to create the right aura of complacency he made the usual reference to his own calling as 'the most accountable and therefore the most acceptable police in the world'. And although he got the largest headlines over an attack on 'bent' lawyers (which showed more the degree of public naivety than any revelatory value), Mark's most serious target was the jury system: 'I cannot think of any other social institution which is protected from rational inquiry because investigation might show that it wasn't doing its job.'

The essence of the police's frustration with juries lies in the fact that half of the people who plead not guilty in front of juries are acquitted. 'Every acquittal', said Mark, 'is a case in which either a guilty man has been allowed to go free or an innocent citizen has been put to the trouble and expense of defending himself.' And then, revealing his own conclusion, he said: ' ... the proportion of those acquittals relating to those whom experienced police officers believe to be guilty is too high to be acceptable.' But Mark failed to point out that with the guilty pleas added, only a quarter of the defendants before the courts are acquitted.

If the efficacy of the law and the courts were to be based on the instincts of 'experienced police officers' and their assumption of the accused's guilt, things would be going a lot further away from the historical presumption of innocence than even the Davies committee had dared to propose. Mark's expression of the police's resentment of transparently concocted defences was understandable, but his lack of sensibility towards the fragile balance of the law makes his judgment very dubious. As Sir Elwyn Jones said in a letter to *The Times* correcting a quotation attributed to him by Mark:

> In 15 years' experience as a Recorder in Wales I had no reason to lose faith in the ability of Welsh juries to see justice was done by convicting the provenly guilty and acquitting the innocent. I only remember one case where I had doubt about the rightness of a conviction. The fact that in a few cases there were what seemed to me to be surprising acquittals is not too high a price to pay for the presumption of innocence.

Seen as a part of a calculated erosion of the rights of the accused and the position of juries, Mark is another polarizing influence in the battle between the Bar and the axis of the police and legal Custodians. Without consulting either

Parliament, the solicitors, or the barristers, the Lord Chancellor agreed with the Attorney-General and the Lord Chief Justice in 1973 that the right of defendants to know the occupation of jurors should be abolished. Basic rights disappear with surprising ease.

The ermine and scarlet, the silk robes, the wigs of varied length according to pecking order, the judge placed in ethereal remoteness – why did the courts choose to stay frozen in this particular period's costume? Was it a subconscious yearning for time to stand still while their dignity was complete, their authority absolute? An eighteenth-century lawyer could return today to an English court to find it – and the law – thoroughly familiar. The precedents set in his time are still dusted off and thought relevant to today's moral dilemmas. Anachronism and insularity have become the law's self-defence.

By making themselves absurd and irrelevant, the courts have also made themselves vulnerable. Plainly dressed despots have subverted the authority of the men in fancy dress. There is now a growing body of law in Britain which governs individual rights but has little, if anything, to do with the courts. It is the law of statute, made not by lawyers but by administrators. It is made to suit the convenience of the machine, and the convenience of the machine is as yielding to the rights of the individual as is a brick wall to the fist of a man. The English Common Law, that anchor of the Anglo-Saxon concept of freedom, is wilting under the infection of this new law.

This development is not sudden. It has been in progress a long time. It has not been particularly subtle or stealthy. As early as 1911 a senior English judge, Sir H. H. Cozens-Hardy, warned: 'Administrative action generally means something done by a man whose name you do not know, sitting at a desk in a government office, very apt to be a despot if free from the interference of the Courts of Justice.' The encroachment on the courts by administrative statutes was already under way, but for worthy enough motives. Between 1905 and 1914, at the period of the first wave of the Welfare State, expenditure on the social services doubled. Even then, as A. J. P. Taylor has pointed out, most of the dealings between the state and the individual involved only the postman or the policeman. Paper-work was minimal. An Englishman didn't need a passport to travel. If he was prosperous enough he was as free as a bird. World War I changed all that, and the freedoms surrendered then have never been won back.

In 1929, Lord Hewart, a bibulous Lord Chief Justice, saw what was happening. In a book called *The New Despotism* he said that the Executive were the champions of 'organized lawlessness', and produced a list of their basic precepts. The first three were:

1. The business of the Executive is to govern.
2. The only persons fit to govern are experts.
3. The experts in the art of government are the permanent officials who, exhibiting an ancient and too much neglected virtue, 'think themselves worthy of great things, being worthy.'

Hewart was incredibly sentient. These are precisely the arguments now used to defend the congenital furtiveness of the Custodians. Hewart saw that the cult of expertise would convince its followers that government 'can be disposed of only if they [the government] were placed above Parliament and beyond the jurisdiction of the courts.' Hewart's book made a big impact, but he later decided that the Welfare State 'justified a powerful Executive'.

The seizure of law-making by the Executive, unimpeded since then, has now taken a new direction. The legislation of the second wave of the Welfare State between 1945 and 1952, like the first, was essentially paternalist. The new statutes are interventionist. The French 'droit administratif' involves statutory laws with built-in judicial safeguards. The contemporary British version omits any similar restraints. Its most ardent architect so far is that strange hybrid of politician, lawyer, and empire-builder, Sir Geoffrey Howe. Only in his mid-forties, Howe is the doctrinal lawyer of the corporate state. He created the divisive and unworkable Industrial Relations Act, but this was a minor step compared to Howe's *tour de force*, the legislation amending the British system to the requirements of Common Market membership.

This change is progressive, eventually transferring fundamental rights to Brussels and the European bureaucracy. Howe therefore becomes as influential as the architects of the Magna Carta. Howe's law shows an affection for statutes and an impatience with courts. His laws are made in ministries. He drafted consumer-protection legislation giving sweeping powers to bureaucrats, leaving the courts as a last resort. It appears to be in a good cause, except that the ministry, the Department of Trade and Industry, is supposed to be policeman, but is also the sponsor of most of the potential offenders. Howe's explanation to *The Sunday Times* was: 'You are not going to solve consumer grievances by mountains of litigation. But what you do is introduce more situations in which litigation is possible at the end of the road, and then this changes the whole atmosphere.' It sounds as though the abstraction of 'atmosphere', with its implied threat is reckoned to be more useful than a court. A lawyer who sets up a bureaucracy to make law as it goes along, regarding courts only as a last resort, is a new kind of lawyer indeed. As the old law is undermined, so too is its constitutional significance. Because it is unwritten, the English Constitution lives only in English law. Usurp that law, and you usurp the Constitution. The Custodians have seen the weakness of the courts, and they have taken the law into their own hands.

British jurists and constitutionalists would do well to mark the words of Edmund Burke: 'It is not what a lawyer tells me I *may* do, but what humanity, reason and justice tell me I *ought* to do.'

Part Two

Misadventures of
Great Britain Ltd

Replacing empire:
Life at the Court of the Corporate Camelot

Television soap-operas are an infallible guide to a country's fantasy life. In Britain they are nearly always nostalgic: the B.B.C.'s quasi-Kipling series on the army in India at the peak of empire; stiff-upper-lip escapes from Colditz Castle in World War II; the suicidal missions of the R.A.F.'s Pathfinders. Even the documentaries follow the same rule: mammoth reconstructions of World War II, echoing the fictional success of Granada's 'Family at War'; biographies of the great battle commanders. There is nothing obscure about the appeal of these programmes – they all hark back not only to a time when Britannia was ruling the waves, but also (perhaps more significantly) to a time when the country was temporarily pulling together and, undoubtedly, at its most courageous.

For a while in the 1960s this backward-looking trend was broken. A new fantasy won peak-time television success: the thrills of big business. 'The Power Game', with its megalomaniac anti-hero John Wilder, managed to make aerospace sexy. Wilder stood for the kind of leadership that the British wanted to believe in. He was a usurper of the old order making it big, and yet at the same time he advanced the cause of True Brit. Towards the end of the series Wilder was given a knighthood, and slipped off his leash into Whitehall – like a wild dog in a chicken coop. It was a metaphor for what was supposed to be happening to the country. As that fantasy collapsed, so the series ended its run.

The life-cycle of 'The Power Game' was a paradigm of the formative years of the British corporate state. Turning the country from a colonial to a commercial power passed from fantasy to fiascos like the Concorde project. From the beginning, True Brit permeated the thinking:

> We are embarking on an adventure of the kind that enabled merchant venturers of the City of London and other cities in time past to win treasure and influence and power for Britain. We go forward in the same spirit of enterprise today. I believe the tide is right, the time is right, the winds are right ...

The winds? That was Harold Wilson, at the Lord Mayor's banquet at the Guildhall in November 1966, four days after he had decided to try to negotiate entry to the Common Market.

It was a strange philosophy for a socialist. The 'merchant venturers' had been unprincipled buccaneers, later exalted as patriots, who pillaged the wealth of the Indies under the British flag. This didn't much matter: they were sanctified by legend, and the British live off their legends. Wilson is prone to such generous interpretations of the past. He likes the operas of Gilbert and Sullivan, and British history as seen through the jingoistic bias of Sir Arthur Bryant. To him the national heritage is a pageant full of gilded and heroic figures.

Now a new race of folk-heroes was in the making, the knights of the Corporate Camelot. Wilson played Merlin, summoning the genie of technology from the cave and offering it to the tired nation as a restorative. To bring this off, there had to be a somersault in social and political attitudes. The Whitehall view of business was like that of the landlord of a whorehouse: it was useful for filling the pocket, but not something you talked about. So it was traumatic for the Custodians to be told that with the empire gone they had better learn the language of the hard sell. It was like trying to turn a spinster into a topless go-go girl.

From 1964, under first Wilson and then Edward Heath, the Custodians have been forced into the embrace of big business. The national interest and the corporate interest have been fused. The traditional separation of government and business has been deliberately dismantled; the boundaries are now obscured. But it is a contract between two inimical *psyches*, the ascetic and the venal. It is also often a contract between two kinds of incompetence: otiose bureaucracy and congenitally sloppy management.

To create this axis between business and government there has been an unparalleled bureaucratic growth. Between 1965 and 1971 the whole structure of Whitehall changed. In 1965 there was one dominant department in the centre, the Treasury, and nineteen subject ministries. By 1971 there was a new three-tier system. At the top the power of the Treasury had been dispersed into three units, the sum greater than the parts: a Civil Service Department as the administrative focus; the Cabinet Office in an expanded form; and the vestigial Treasury. Instead of diminishing the grasp of the Custodians by ending the monolithic role of the Treasury, this system made the political and administrative links even more arcane, especially in the Cabinet Office.

There was an equally portentous development in the second tier, the creation of three mega-ministries, the Department of Trade and Industry; the Department of the Environment, and the Department of Health and Social Security. Between them these three have a staff of 170,000. They have eclipsed the old 'imperial' departments, the Foreign Office and the Defence Ministry. They also overshadow the third tier of minor ministries.

This concentration of power evolved through a bewildering chain-reaction of departmental title-changes and mergers. Officials controlling complex and accident-prone projects were shunted from one organizational chart to another. The 'management' of the North Sea oil contracts, for example, ran through three different ministries in six years. Each time the line of command became more evanescent.

To try to compensate for the inadequacy of the Custodians, specialist businessmen were drafted into Whitehall. These men were appalled by what they found. The ministry buildings, most of them monuments built at the peak of empire, were – like their inhabitants – marooned out of their time. Some had become grandiose slums. On the walls were the murals of rampant True Brit, panoramas of imperial conquest. Yet the toilets were so primitive that senior staff could be seen walking the corridors carrying their own private towels and soap, kept furtively from thieving hands in locked desk drawers, along with secret files.

This petty, spinsterish hoarding of things like soap and the biscuits to go with afternoon tea is imbued in the Whitehall mentality. Sir Richard Meyjes, a director of Shell who served for a while as an adviser, recalls: 'The financial system dates back to Samuel Pepys. It was designed to stop kings spending money on mistresses.'

Under the elaborately formalized mannerisms was a feline talent for in-fighting. A stiletto could be planted in the back with surgical precision and the victim could never tell, from those saturnine faces, where it had come from. Jealous of their power, assured by their illusions, and hostile to the intruding professionals, the Custodians sabotaged, neutralized or by-passed the attempts to implant a grasp of modern management. The Department of Economic Affairs, set up by Wilson to provide the economic expertise which the Treasury lacked, had to be abandoned after the Custodians froze it out. Nothing could have been a clearer expression of the power of their club: either the game was played by their rules or it was not played at all. No matter that the rules were obsolete.

The outsiders were beaten by the ruthless use of negative power. Positive decision-making, especially that involving anything innovative, was too conspicuous and too perilous to careers depending on the automatic and secure pecking-order of seniority. Lord Balogh, one of the outside advisers who had persistently tried to sound the alarm about the North Sea oil licences, commented ruefully: 'Sins of commission are feared. The deadly vice of omission gets further promotion.'

Over a decade only one graft from outside has really 'taken' and that – significantly – is from the same blood-group. In an attempt at least to monitor the Custodians, Heath installed a 'Think Tank' (Kennedyesque terms are still fashionable in Whitehall). And to run it he chose one of the few men in business who could play the game by the rules of the Custodians, since he was virtually one of them himself: Victor, the third Baron Rothschild.

Unlike the French branch of the family, the British Rothschilds have a liberal bent. After wartime service in military intelligence, Victor Rothschild ran the research department at Shell. He is a natural scientist, banker, polymath – and a very superior person. In the high noon of Whitehall he could out-draw and out-shoot the most mendacious mandarin. And the way he went about re-cruiting his staff of fifteen great thinkers is a classic example of tapping the elitist conduit. Rothschild has described it to *The Sunday Times* with candour:

> I sometimes go to the Barbados, and since Dick Ross told me he knew a very good man on one of these sugar boards called Hector Hawkins, I made it my business to have rum punch with him – perhaps two – and I thought Hector was very nice and very good so I asked if he would make a sacrifice and join me in the Cabinet Office.

The scene is pure Somerset Maugham: the porch at sundown, the colonial sugar plantations, the clink of ice in the tall glasses, the casual assessment of character as the punch warms the stomach, the value system of 'very nice and very good'. As one of the transactions of True Brit it is better than fiction. Somebody not in the know would have said, and it would have been a lack of couth fatal to his chances,

'Barbados' – not '*the* Barbados'.

Lord Rothschild said that he had chosen another member of the Think Tank, the son of a fellow peer, 'because his father's a friend of mine and I asked his father if he might like it.' With that kind of grapevine working for it, the Think Tank easily ingratiated itself into the system. It gave the Custodians no trouble: it was a mirror of themselves.

One way of trying to make insiders out of outsiders is to give them a title. Peerages and knighthoods are seldom given for selfless duty to the Crown, more often for services rendered. Brasher businessmen are shamelessly importuning, especially if they are colonials. The Canadian owner of *The Times* and *Sunday Times*, Roy Thomson, was disarmingly vigorous in his supplications to Harold Macmillan, but in the end he got a peerage for being brave enough to save *The Times* from bankruptcy.

In 1966 Harold Wilson told a friend (later to be a baroness): 'I hope in the next week or two to abolish the whole political honours system ... I don't know whether my colleagues will agree.' Evidently they didn't. Wilson became profligate with his patronage. Where the Tories dispensed titles in return for donations to party funds, Wilson handed them out to the new folk-heroes of True Brit. He founded the Court of the Corporate Camelot.

A typical candidate was Donald Stokes, a man with the smile of a car salesman, which is what he is. Stokes was picked by Wilson as the man to rationalize the foundering car industry. The American-owned satellites of Ford and General Motors were eating away the markets of under-capitalized British dynasties turning out uncompetitive models. Under Wilson's patronage Stokes carried out a shotgun marriage of the old marques like Austin, Morris, Rover, Jaguar, Daimler, and Leyland. This ragbag became British Leyland, and Stokes got first a knighthood and then a peerage. He also got a continuing headache.

Under Wilson and Heath corporate knighthoods and peerages showered into boardrooms. In every honours list there are an average of ten corporate knighthoods. At the summit of Camelot it doesn't stop with a simple peerage. Lord Cole, a frozen-food tycoon, became a Knight Grand Cross of the Order of the British Empire for a particularly painful act in the service of True Brit: the plucking from the ashes of Rolls Royce.

But these politically donated titles cannot buy admission to the inner sanctums of the Custodians. One of the most ruthless company surgeons, an exemplar of his order, is Sir Arnold Weinstock. His charisma bewitched two Prime Ministers, who sponsored his company, G.E.C., through a series of mergers, to become the ninth largest in Britain, with a net annual profit in 1973 of £92·4m.

Weinstock is a Jew, which, together with his contempt for the True Brit style of doing business, loads the dice against him in places where the old guard rules. He was nominated by friends for membership of Brooks's Club in St James's, one of the original cells of Custodian power, founded in 1764. These clubs use an anonymous method of voting to select new members: that of white balls placed in a box. If one or more black balls appear in the box the applicant has been 'blackballed', a symbolic rejection with particularly unsubtle implications. Brooks's, a fortress of white supremacy, rejected Weinstock. It was not ready to accept the scourge of True Brit.

Knighthoods – and acceptance into the clubs – fall as an automatic right to the Custodians in Whitehall once they reach senior rank. As Snow said of Hector Rose, they might not mean much outside, but they are a perquisite of office earned simply by seniority, and kept for life, whatever fiascos follow in their wake. Whitehall knights look with disdain on the dilution of their order by the Corporate Camelot. There is no way of gate-crashing their fortress, even if the outer battlements are not what they were.

And so there is this immutable cleavage between two cultures, supposedly joined in the contract to re-package True Brit but fundamentally living in separate worlds according to inimical codes. Unwittingly, the ambit of the Custodians has been enlarged to a degree which is barely comprehended. Incompetent power is as dangerous as irresponsible power; perhaps it is even more dangerous because it might always precipitate the kind of collapse for which, as Baroness Sharp warned, others are waiting in the wings. Her warning is not fanciful.

Between 1968 and 1970, the nadir of the Wilson regime, a cabal of disenchanted businessmen met frequently to consider a *putsch*. They had for a while the tacit support of two newspaper proprietors, Cecil King of the *Daily Mirror* (circulation 4½m.) and Lord Thomson of *The Times* (circulation 400,000). It was *The Times* which in 1968 favoured a coalition government. This group never really coalesced into an organized threat, but its existence indicates how readily British businessmen believe that politics is too serious a matter to be left to politicians. Among its number were the chairmen of the second- and fourth-ranking industrial giants, Shell and Imperial Chemical Industries; two peers from the outer non-executive fringes of the Custodians, the Lords Crowther and Shawcross; Lord Cole, chairman of Unilever, the fifth-ranking firm; and a recording-company tycoon.

Their choice for Prime Minister (without public consent) was Lord Robens, chairman of the nationalized coal industry and a favourite in the court of the Corporate Camelot. *The Times*'s idea of a coalition government had disastrous precedents. Secretly the businessmen's cabal used the term 'Emergency Government'. But there was something crazy about the plot. It represented strong business nous but a great deal of political naivety. Its planning was gauche, the planners more sure of what was going wrong than how to put it right. And there was one essentially right-wing conviction behind it: True Brit was in jeopardy not because of the Custodians but because of industrial anarchy.

The history of industrial relations was appalling, but as culpable as the unions were the sloppy managements of the

League of Gentlemen and the maladroit work of the Custodians. The putative coup faded away, ending with a desultory lunch at Brown's Hotel in 1970. Lord Crowther, who was then chairman of the Royal Commission on the British Constitution, said dolorously that he saw no future for British democracy, nor could he tell what would take its place.

In fact, the Constitution had already been pre-empted. The marriage of government and business, and the accretion of Custodian power that followed it, has swept away the checks and balances and severely diminished individual rights and freedoms.

As the mega-ministries were taking shape in Whitehall, the same trend was axiomatic in British business. 'Conglomeration' was in fashion, and enthusiastically endorsed by government. Britain is far more tolerant of business monopoly than the U.S.A., and much more dominated by it. By 1970 half of the country's net national output came from the 100 largest manufacturing firms. In the U.S.A. the top 100 companies produce only a third of the national output. If this trend continues, 90 per cent of British business will be in the hands of the top 100 companies by the year 2000. Already, just 9 per cent of British industry accounts for 94 per cent of all corporate trading profits.

In the U.S.A., the Federal Trade Commission estimates that if a market can be regulated so that its four largest producers share no more than 40 per cent of it, retail prices in that market can be cut by at least a quarter. And yet in Britain there are more than 150 markets where half or more of the business is in the hands of one firm or group.

Between 1966 and 1968, the seminal period in government-sponsored mergers in Britain, the money spent per year in take-overs jumped from £535m. to £2,312m. The creation of both the corporate giants and the Whitehall mega-ministries reflects the same idea: bigness equals effectiveness. If True Brit was not to be emasculated in the international markets, it had to be able to shape up to the giants.

But this presupposed two things: a correct choice of the right businesses to be in, and that there was a supply of the management skills to carry it off. Both assumptions were wrong. The most direct result of the cult of bigness was that the mistakes got bigger. Many of the largest companies, like English Electric, Vickers, and Rolls Royce, were not as formidable or as secure as they seemed. And in the lower levels of British industry there was many an unwary board sleeping on the job. For those with the eye to see it, the time was right for ruthless opportunism.

9 Busting up the League of Gentlemen: the Hustlers, the Strippers, and the Importance of Not Being Wet

'The stock-jobbers can ruin men silently; they undermine and impoverish them, and fiddle them out of their money by the strange, unheard-of engines of interest, discount, transfers, tallies, debentures, shares, projects, and the devil and all of figures and hard names.' – *Contemporary chronicler on the City of London, 1968*

The British dislike that Teutonic streak which makes a good corporate hatchet-man. This is not to say that they are not themselves tricky. But they will seldom turn a crooked hand to the service of anything so impersonal as the body corporate. It is self that they serve best – though they would have you believe anything but. This helps to explain a common confusion in the minds of foreigners who get tangled with the British businessman: how can people with such fancy footwork get the country into such a hell of a mess? Surely all that cunning ought to pay off? It does, but only for them.

The ambition of the British businessman has a low cut-out point. Having made enough money for his own comfort, he is content to coast along in a half-hearted way. He assembles his perquisites, the company car, the chauffeur, the country cottage, the golf-club membership, a boat, and the numerous smaller luxuries of the expense account – all the symbols of success. He does not, beyond this, flourish his wealth or tax his energies. For an average member of the League of Gentlemen this life is his ceiling.

He will look with distaste at corporate gangsterdom on the International Telephone and Telegraph scale, not because of the means but because of the ends. The British gentleman is best at being a privateer, not a hired hand. He has his own opaque code, which can be summarized as: 'it takes one to catch one; as long as we stick together nobody gets caught.'

Although the running of many large industrial firms has passed from the founding dynasties into the hands of managers answerable to shareholders, this has not altered the British belief that company directors need only to belong to the League of Gentlemen to qualify. More than two-thirds of British business executives went to an independent school. This is more important for the moulding of their *persona* than for providing relevant skills. Only 8 per cent have been to a business school, and only 35 per cent have any professional qualification.

As a career with the Custodians is a birthright of the cream of the Oxbridge classics scholars, so a place in a British boardroom is regarded as the birthright of the less brilliant pupils, the members of the League of Gentlemen. There is also the question of nepotism. Despite the advent of the managers, nearly a third of the top 120 public companies in Britain have boards loaded with members of the founding family, or are under the patriarchal control of their creators. This combination of surviving dynasties and executives chosen according to their old school ties presents a stiff resistance to anyone believing that a business school and professional training are enough to earn a place at the top.

It was this system that the knights of the Corporate Camelot were supposed to break. They had little chance. The gentlemen are as deeply entrenched in their citadel as are the Custodians. But what a different kind of citadel it is.

The City of London, the British financial cockpit since the first merchants and bankers set up business there centuries ago, is the most lawless square mile in the country. It is virtually a nation-state on its own, with its own Lord Mayor, its own police force, its own clubs, and its own ancient rituals and modern rackets. As a financial centre its influence outstrips that of the country itself. It has more securities listed and a higher market capitalization than all other European markets put together. But it has never been a paragon of financial behaviour.

City bankers invented paper money and swindles on a global scale. They created the South Sea Bubble, in which a Prime Minister, Walpole, bought in at 130, sold at 1,000 and watched thousands ruined as the chimera collapsed. By the morals of the eighteenth century this was unexceptionable. 'Bribery in all its forms', noted an observer, 'was as necessary in public affairs as are shells in war.' This belief lives on, though the methods are now much more sophisticated. About the only area of modern technology which the League of Gentlemen have happily embraced is the corporate swindle. Like the furtive pact of sodomy in the public-school dormitory, dirty tricks in the City enjoy a tacit consent as part of the way of life – so long as nobody blabs.

The line between ethics and crime in British business has always been hazy. The ethos of the club prefers loose and unwritten codes rather than open and explicit policing, self-regulation rather than imposed law. This springs directly from the double-standard of the class system: gentlemen can be trusted, others need laws.

Many large businesses have disreputable origins; a liquor fortune may have been built out of bootlegging, or a textile industry from nineteenth-century social crimes like sweated child labour. After their early delinquent phase the clever operators learn to cover their tracks and build an ivory tower for the next generation. In the City of London, one generation's bandits beget the next generation's pillars of society; the parvenu melts into the paragon. This requires a high degree of cynicism and hypocrisy, and the British are not underprovided with either.

As long as the compact of the League of Gentlemen holds together, it guarantees succession from one generation to another, hoarding the wealth and concealing the methods of gaining it.

At the age of 32, James Derrick Slater was having a touch of bad luck. Rising fast as the wheeler-dealer sales director under the as yet un-knighted Donald Stokes, Slater had been selling trucks to Spaniards when he was struck down by a virus. The taut, driven Slater was no gentleman; he worked too hard and he had needed something to slow him down. The bug did it.

For convalescence, Stokes ordered him to the seaside resort of Bournemouth, where the genteel spend their twilight years being wheeled in bath chairs along cliffs, wrapped in tartan rugs. It was a boring place for a hotshot sales director to be stuck in. As a diversion, Slater started looking at stockbroker reports on public companies. Then came the Message. Some companies seemed to Slater curiously undervalued, often because their assets were marked down artificially low. And companies recuperating from losses were, he thought, revalued far too slowly by the market.

Slater decided to direct his personal insight into a new kind of alchemy. The Message begat the System. He had a modest £2,000 in savings. In one year the System turned the £2,000 into £50,000 by astute buying of undervalued stocks. It was a better way of making money than selling trucks. Magnanimously, Slater had let some of his friends in on the System. It ran so well that, to the great regret of Stokes, he set up business on his own as an investment adviser.

Slater had done more than find a way of getting rich quick. He had spotted the vulnerability of the League of Gentlemen. In his first year as a loner he made another £75,000. But that was only a beginning.

Slater was noticed by a London evening newspaper, which included him in a series of profiles of rising young businessmen. Another operator selected by the paper was an insurance broker called Peter Walker, three years younger than Slater.

Walker and Slater both left school at sixteen. Neither had any of the gloss of the League of Gentlemen. Slater's father was a builder, Walker's a grocer. Both came from north London suburbs and had flat suburban accents. But there was a difference in outlook. Walker had strong political ambitions, and was in a group of young Tories who wanted to move their party off the grouse-moors. Slater had the kind of Tory sympathies of anyone who suddenly has capital to conserve, but he was a monomaniac, in the grip of his own discovery. None the less, Slater and Walker were as pre-destined as partners as Procter and Gamble.

Their connexion came when Walker organized a dinner for all the go-getters featured by the evening paper. Slater explained the System to Walker. The young Tory had financial links in the City that Slater lacked. Like a couple of raiders mining the ramparts before an assault, the two combined talents and formed Slater, Walker Ltd. It was 1964. With an unintended irony they were setting out to achieve by manipulation of the 'market forces' and for their own ends what Harold Wilson was planning to do by state intervention: bust up the League of Gentlemen.

To Walker there was a political rationale, the updating of free enterprise, as well as the more venal pleasure; for Slater such philosophizing was irrelevant. Like most commercial banditry, the success of the Slater, Walker assault depended on the somnolence of their victims. When Slater spotted an undervalued asset, it meant that somebody who should have known better was ignorant of the value of what they were sitting on. So it was with the partnership's first coup.

They found a near-derelict clothing firm called, as luck would have it, H. Lotery. The share price was well below the nominal break-up asset value. With £700,000 of mostly borrowed money, they took over Lotery and turned it into the shell of Slater, Walker Ltd. In the process the company's hidden asset, a central London office building, was sold for nearly £2m. With land and property values escalating,

Slater, Walker set the pattern for a new sport: asset stripping. Companies with sluggish earnings were bought up,
cut down to a viable size and the stripped-off assets sold at
high profit. It was remarkably easy, once the trick was
learned, and it showed how comatose were many of the
boardrooms populated by the League of Gentlemen. While
they were out on the grouse-moors or golf courses, the
gimlet eye of Slater cased the company records. Then the
predators moved in.

By 1968, asset-stripping was too conspicuous, even
notorious. The gentlemen, now wise to the game, called
Slater a jackal. Walker was getting sensitive about his
political image. He was inside Edward Heath's cabal of
planners for the new Conservatism, an apostle of business
reform. He didn't want to be tarnished as a wrecker rather
than a builder. By then both he and Slater were multi-
millionaires. They could afford to look for something more
elegant.

And so the strippers became bankers. With more fancy
footwork they bought a small bank, Ralli Brothers, and
transformed it into an international investment network.
With this under way Slater, Walker took a symbolic step.
They moved offices from the West End of London through
the gates and into the City of London. They then began the
complex process of selling off their industrial interests –
more than £40m. worth – and spinning them off into
partly owned satellites. From share speculations they moved
to stripping, from stripping to industrial conglomerates,
from that into banking. Each move had been ahead of the
game or, as one Slater Walker protégé put it: 'It's a sort of
mirror-trick, trying to keep ahead of the dirty word'.

By 1970 Slater and Walker were each reckoned to have
made their first £10m.

There is a way in Britain of defining a particular kind of
lassitude when it goes with an effete nature. It is called 'wet'.
There are wet people and wet behaviour. In this sense the

antonym of wet is not dry, but hard.

The absence of Teutonic dedication in British corporate managers is regarded as wet by men who would rather be hard. Wetness is not a failing of Peter Walker or of Jim Slater, nor of Edward Heath.

As he watched the shambles of British business, Heath saw too much wetness and too many wets. Edward Heath is not a sympathetic man; he has an emetic laugh, he is so bad at small talk that he walks around at parties in his own portable limbo. There is a certain insouciance in his manner that can chill the most convivial company. He is a bit of a Boy Scout and, in spite of his ample girth, an enemy of getting 'soft'. Wetness drives him crazy.

With Heath's blessing, Peter Walker took his gunslinging style into government. He had made himself rich beyond the dreams of a lower-class surburban boyhood, and far richer than Heath, who was from a similar background. But some of Walker's golden touch seems to have rubbed off on Heath. Between 1965 and 1968, when Slater, Walker took off, Heath did remarkably well with a modest investment of £8,000; just how well he didn't say. But if Slater could turn £2,000 into £50,000 in a year, Heath – with the right advice – wouldn't be badly off. He confirmed that he left the management of his money to others, and no doubt Walker was one of those who obliged.

The outward evidence of Heath's good fortune was two yachts, Morning Cloud II at £22,000, replaced by Morning Cloud III at £45,000. Getting wet the Heath way meant hard, rugged sailing. This was made clear at the Tory party conference in 1970, a few months after he took the country's helm: 'Our purpose is to bring our fellow citizens to recognize that they must be responsible for the consequences of their own actions and to learn that no one will stand between them and the results of their own free choice.'

With Walker at his elbow, Heath decided that the country needed a rigorous course in the art of Not Being Wet. Looking with a mean eye at British industry, John Davies warned: 'The government will not help lame ducks across ponds or assist a morass of subsidized incompetence.'

The League of Gentlemen couldn't believe what they were hearing: a *Tory* government abandoning the cosy compact of state and business, prepared to allow the weakest to go to the wall? And since the most vulnerable of the weak were the totems of True Brit, how could Heath be so hard of heart? They needn't have worried. Faced with the imminent collapse of Rolls Royce, the most illustrious of those totems, Heath relented. The art of being non-wet did not extend to allowing Rolls Royce to wipe itself out. Similar somersaults followed. Heath was as prone to the hallucinations of True Brit as anyone.

If propping up the superannuated symbols of True Brit was *not* wet, what was? *The Times*, that erstwhile supporter of government by tycoon, had its own idea. In the course of a eulogy of Herr Willy Brandt, the West German Chancellor, it said:

> As nationally we are going through a wet mood, we are lucky not to have a wet Prime Minister ... the German people, with their serious and authoritarian family life and educational system are a well-disciplined people. The British educational system was never as highly disciplined, and what elements of discipline it used to have are for better or worse now much reduced ...

It was a long time since anyone had dared to suggest to the British that German 'discipline' was an inspiration. But *The Times* had two favourite images of British wetness: students and trade unions. Certainly nobody could describe the German treatment of either students or unions as forgiving. If only, mused the Teutons on *The Times*, we could be like that ...

While Slater, Walker and the Hustlers were screwing the gentlemen, whom had the gentlemen been screwing?

The sheep in the City of London are the small investors.

In spite of the growth of unit trusts, the fleecing of the sheep got so bad that – against all the trends – the number of shareholders in Britain actually declined, at the rate of 5 per cent a year. The contest between lay ignorance and professional cunning is too unequal. Small investors are the cannon-fodder of the Hustlers. These investors rely on shares to subsidize meagre pensions. They are inexpert in the new arts of the market; they have no way of reading signs and playing dirty tricks. Their interests are supposed to be in the care of the Stock Exchange Council. But, like all the instruments of the League of Gentlemen, the Council is a case of the robbers policing the robbers. It is composed entirely of the self-sustaining clique of brokers and jobbers who put their own interests above that of the public.

There is no watchdog with anything like the teeth of the Securities and Exchange Committee in the U.S.A., as fallible as even that is. The surge of take-overs and mergers made insider-dealing, outlawed in the U.S.A., a lucrative game in the City of London. Anybody with inside knowledge – which means the professional analysts – read the signs of an incipient bid and could make a killing if they were unscrupulous. Rich pickings were made by executives inside the companies involved.

This became so flagrant that the gentlemen set up a Panel to monitor take-overs and mergers. Its methods were risible. The ethics of the club were at work again. The Panel's inquiries were conducted, said its director-general, in an atmosphere of 'polite exchanges'. And, giving the whole game away, he added: 'We probably catch the less intelligent, not the man who has set out to act dishonestly and has covered his tracks well.'

An even truer glimpse of the tortured ethics of the City came from Sir Martin Wilkinson, the chairman of the Stock Exchange, who allowed that insider dealing was 'no better than stealing' but said that the public was outraged by it not because some people had made a pile, but because they themselves hadn't.

'Keeping ahead of the dirty word', the two original Hustlers themselves had the nerve to complain about the legalized lawlessness in the City. Insider dealing, said Slater, was giving business a bad name. Walker was also vocally disapproving.

When Walker joined the Heath Cabinet in 1970 he sold his Slater, Walker shares, but the company kept his name and the two moved in parallel. Although still not overtly political, Slater supported the Tories from company funds, at the rate of about £15,000 a year. Edward Heath, according to Slater, was 'the personification of meritocracy in politics'. Heath was certainly good for business, and business was good for Slater. But Slater and Walker went one stage further than that: what was good for business was good for Britain.

At the heart of non-wetness is a belief in the national virtue of making a fast buck. The Tories should, said Slater, 'generate an atmosphere in which success and profit in business are regarded as important and in the interest of the country.' Lord Stokes, still desperately encumbered with his wayward car giant, sang the same song. The endemic lack of ambition, the feigned diffidence towards money, the social snobbery against the Hustlers – these were the traits of wetness which Heath and the Hustlers abhorred. 'I think', said Slater, 'Slater, Walker played a part in the reformation of British industry and to this extent we have certainly contributed to the country's welfare, as well as in the more direct material sense.'

Turning his hand to an equally glib self-justification, Walker said: 'Capitalism should not be regarded as the means for a few to get rich.' And to an audience of assembled industrialists in London in January 1973, he laid out the rules of non-wet management with the simple fervour of a Boy Scout:

Be efficient and make a profit for Britain;
Don't pollute;
Look after the workers;

Don't cheat;
Uphold the national objectives.

And, he might have added, take a cold shower every morning.

Walker called this threadbare code 'The New Capitalism'. The Hustlers desperately wanted the British to regard making money as *acceptable*. But those who did have plenty of money didn't want to talk about it, and those who didn't weren't concerned with niceties like whether or not business was socially taboo; they would simply have liked to see some of the money coming their way.

Perhaps why the Hustlers craved so openly for a kind of ethical acceptance was that they still felt excluded from the club, even after their noble work in the reformation of derelict industry. They were right, as Slater discovered in the most galling way.

He had built a company with earnings of nearly £20m. a year, but he wanted something better. He dreamed of a new style *banque d'affaires*, a kind of multi-national financial empire which British entry into the Common Market made logical. With such a coup, Slater would be king of the City. And it came within his grasp.

Slater spent six weeks secretly negotiating with Sir Kenneth Keith, chairman of the merchant bank Hill Samuel. Keith is a man of two parts. The bottom part has the stout thighs of a land-owning squire, the top part the rapier mind of a veteran manipulator. Keith had what Slater lacked: a subtlety of style. He had engineered many take-overs, but without attracting the displeasure of the club. He and his bank had the *gravitas* which Slater knew he needed.

To get it, Slater was prepared to be humble. He accepted a deal in which the Slater, Walker name would disappear into a joint empire, and in which he would play second fiddle to Keith. It didn't seem like the old Slater style; some wondered whether he was losing his touch, even whether he was ill.

Ironically, it fell to Walker as the Industry Minister to decide whether the Slater–Hill Samuel deal should be referred to the Monopolies Commission, or allowed to go ahead. Aware of his embarrassment, Walker deputed the decision to a deputy who, not without taking flak, gave the green light. Together the Slater–Keith operation would have had gross assets of £1,500m., making it the equal in international capability of First National City of New York. But it was not to be. As they got down to stitching the two outfits together, Slater and Keith discovered in each other serious divergencies of style. Slater was not a natural second man, and Keith was too dominant to move sideways.

When the deal was called off, there were audible sighs of relief from the League of Gentlemen. Slater was to them a cad, a bounder, an upstart, an outsider – not the kind of chap who ought to be allowed in the Club, whatever the size of his bank balance. But the gentlemen were less pleased by Walker's next caper. Trickery in the City had become so bad, he said, that there would have to be new and much tougher company laws. Many people saw the cynicism of his own role – reversal. And expert observers felt that creating laws did not automatically stop lawlessness. The artful dodges were too ingrained, too recondite, to be deterred by what was, after all, cosmetic politics.

The Slater, Walker raids have meaning as a reflection of the political effort to smash the hold and expose the methods of the gentlemen. Slater and Walker enriched themselves rather than the country, but at the start their freebooting piracy was more disruptive to the old order than the government policies, which, instead of spilling blood in the City, built the axis between finance and industry on one side and a gullible but omnipotent bureaucracy on the other. In the end, though, the two pirates – like so many other erstwhile challengers of the British system – were prepared to stand on their heads to be accepted by that system.

Walker grabbed to the full Heath's invitation to bring non-wet dealing into government, but he had to try to make it palatable with the disingenuous gloss of 'The New Capitalism'. Slater, a much more private person, rode thoughtfully in the back of his Bentley calculating the steps to his metamorphosis as an international banker, rewriting his own history as he went. Both are like a couple of small boys who have been caught poaching on the estate and then marry into the owner's family. They can drink a Sunday morning sherry with the Hunt, but they can never – however much they crave it – be accepted as one of Them. This is the British way, and it hasn't changed.

10 Oil from troubled waters: a case history in management by Custodian

The axis created in Whitehall between industry and government put major industrial policy into the hands of the Custodians. Ostensibly the decision-makers were supposed to be politicians. Actually the complexity of the issues and the uncertain tenancy of governments meant that the interpretation of any situation provided by the bureaucrats predetermined the political decision. Since this interpretation was being provided by men who were themselves out of their depth, in a commercial atmosphere which they found distasteful, the process was not only undemocratic but highly accident-prone.

The North Sea oil bonanza is definitive as a case history of Great Britain Ltd in action. In six years the management of the oil exploration went through several phases in the fumbling escalation of the central bureaucracies.

The North Sea is an inverted wedge of water at its widest between Norway and the outer Scottish islands, and ending in a narrow 30-mile-wide spout between England and northern France. Its depth at the northern end is over 400 feet; at the southern end it is half that. The North Sea forms a funnel for winds and storms: it is one of the most treacherous stretches of water in the world. It is relatively shallow because it is a part of the European Continental Shelf; that shelf is traversed by basins, platforms and trenches. There are similar basins in Russia, North Africa, Australia, West Texas, Oklahoma, and Western Canada. Wherever they occur, these basins have one thing in common. There is a high chance that they will bear oil in commercial quantities.

Offshore rigs in the Texas gulf and the West Indies are to the North Sea what the Ritz in Paris is to a fur-trapper's cabin. Even when geologists began to look at the North Sea seriously as a possible oil-field, in the 1950s, the idea of anyone getting a rig out into that mendacious water and staying alive long enough to sink a bore-hole seemed a little unhinged. But oil prospectors these days are not so easily discouraged. The world's supplies are running out; Britain had no fields of her own, and most of her supplies came from the politically precarious zones of Africa and the Middle East.

In 1958 Britain and other countries bordering the North Sea signed a Convention apportioning shares of the Continental Shelf, carving up on the maps what they all hoped would prove to be an undersea gusher. And since Britain covers the whole western perimeter of the North Sea hers was the lion's share, west of a line bisecting it from north to south. There was no guarantee either that oil was there, or, if it was, that it would be worth drilling for, so that sheer acreage was not in itself a key to riches. Holland, with a small slice of the deal, hit a rich gas field.

In 1964 British policy for exploring the North Sea for gas and oil was drawn up in Whitehall. By then, the world's major oil companies had warmed to the North Sea. But in Whitehall nobody had any experience of oil prospecting. The British share of the oil business was relatively modest: there was British Petroleum, 48 per cent owned by the British government, and Shell, an Anglo–Dutch company in which the British stake was 40 per cent. The international oil business was dominated by the Americans.

So far as there was anything clear about British policy, it was that the country ought to do as well out of the exploitation of her own resources as she knew how. To put it simply, could the British be as smart as the Arabs? More than that, could they be as smart as the British oil-men who were used to dealing with Arabs? The negotiating skills acquired via an English upper-class education followed by years of coping with the cunning of the kasbah were for-midable.

When negotiations opened, the Petroleum Division of the Ministry of Power had three administrators, no techni-cal staff, two junior-grade 'executive'-rank civil servants, and three clerks. When the oil-men walked in it was a meeting of experience and innocence, of savvy and naivety. The prize was an energy source worth billions. From the start the battle was unequal.

Instead of dealing like men sitting on a fortune, the Custodians behaved like mendicants. They were made to believe that they had to *persuade* the oil-men to start pros-pecting. The oil-men made a melodrama out of the prob-lems of the North Sea. They said that exploration would be dangerous and costly and that the technology was unproven. There was enough truth in this to make it stick, but at that point the oil-men held all the cards. The ministry had no staff geologists nor any other relevant technical knowledge.

The terms the oil-men won were anything but onerous. There was a royalty rate of $12\frac{1}{2}$ per cent; a down payment of £6,250 per block of 100 square miles covering six years, followed by an annual payment of £10,000 per block, rising to a maximum of £72,500. Within that time-scale the highest rate applied only well into the life of a proven strike; barren blocks could be surrendered within the six-year period. A fruitful block could be held on those terms for forty-six years: there was no break clause, no scope for re-negotiation.

The oil companies' psychological warfare was masterly. As well as making the ministry feel grateful that they were ready to take up the burden, they played another card, abetted by the Arabists in the Foreign Office. If the British terms were too stiff, they suggested, the Arabs would take the hint and follow suit. This deeply impressed the civil servants, who were very anxious not to instruct Arabs how to impoverish oil companies.

At first, the reputation of the North Sea seemed to be

borne out. Three drilling rigs were lost. Thirteen men were drowned. A new kind of rig had to be designed. In December 1965 a British Petroleum drill hit gas at a site thirty-five miles off the coast of Yorkshire. Between then and the end of 1967 three other major gas-fields were found a little to the south. These gas strikes transformed British energy prospects: 90 per cent of British gas now comes from the North Sea; since 1967 the country's consumption of gas has more than doubled. But gas was, after all, only the *hors d'oeuvre*. Finding it indicated that the chances of hitting oil were good, and that was why the oil-men were there in the first place.

In 1969 Phillips Petroleum hit oil inside the Norwegian sector of the North Sea, under 230 feet of water in a field called Ekofisk. Although the Ekofisk strike confounded oil-company pessimism about viable oil-fields, the Custodians were becoming alarmed that – after three rounds of licence negotiations – interest in the North Sea seemed to be falling off. By 1969 the Petroleum Division in Whitehall had grown modestly to a total of twenty-one, including three technicians. Nothing had been done about providing independent geological information until 1967. The Custodians had been content to rely on what the oil companies told them. And as the scent of strikes grew stronger in the nostrils of the oil-men, the more they increased their scepticism in public.

With the coming of the Heath government in 1970, the Petroleum Division for the first time came under the eye of a professional oil-man. The timing was crucial, because the civil servants were thoroughly taken in by the gloomy prognoses of the companies. In a Whitehall reorganization, the Division was included in the new Department of Trade and Industry, whose minister was John Davies, a former managing director of Shell. But Davies failed to grasp how gullible his senior officials were being in negotiating with the oil companies. The ministry's policy was in the hands of Sir Robert Marshall, and during the six years of the Labour government they had resisted all attempts to stiffen the terms of the contracts, although there were already suspicions that a fortune was virtually being given away.

In 1970, as Davies took over, Marshall and his staff had been mousetrapped. Their case for generous contracts was that they wanted the resources tapped rapidly. But, even though the Ekofisk strike indicated rich oil sources, the civil servants had panicked into believing that the companies were losing interest. All three previous rounds of oil licences were what the ministry called 'discretionary'. Companies or consortia had to satisfy the ministry of their suitability, and they got the blocks on the original 1964 terms. Nobody had proposed following the American practice of competitive auctions. Instead of parting with licences for peanuts, this would have set a realistic market price for blocks of the North Sea.

But by 1971 the panic in the ministry was so acute that they decided to release 436 blocks for tender, including most of the promising fields. Almost as an afterthought, fifteen of the blocks were put up for auction as an experiment; the rest went on the 1964 terms. The auctioned blocks were mixed to include five reckoned to be poor, five moderate, and five promising. Experience had shown that 'poor' blocks could yield strikes and 'good' blocks turn out to be barren.

What then happened ought to have been the terminal indictment of nine years of peanut-vending. Of the 436 blocks offered, 267 were taken up on the 'discretionary' basis and produced for the ministry £3m. The fifteen auctioned blocks produced £37m. On a straight extrapolation of the market price established by the auction, all the blocks would have been worth £750m. instead of the £40m. raised. Even allowing that there was simply not that much money around for oil exploration, and that some blocks were more attractive than others, two things were painfully clear – the best part of the oil- and gas-fields had been as good as given away, and in the panic far more blocks had been allowed to go than should have done.

It was a gigantic and costly miscalculation. But Sir Robert Marshall and his staff were oblivious: they went ahead and compounded the fiasco. The 'discretionary' contracts were allowed to go ahead, although by the time the auction result was in, no commitments had been made other than the advertised invitations. To have revised the terms then would have been, in Sir Robert's words, 'a breach of faith'. This was the language of a man playing a game of bridge in a Pall Mall club, rather than of a man just caught as the victim of a confidence trick.

Had Davies grasped what was going on? All the ministers who had been, from 1964, nominally responsible for North Sea oil policy had been swept along by their Custodians, either over-trusting or negligent. Asked later if he had told Davies about the implications of the auction, Sir Robert was evasive: 'The minister was informed at once of the results of the auction. He knew that action was proceeding on the applications of the discretionary system. *He was not specifically reminded of the receipts from initial payments.*' (My italics.)

Thus the nimble side-step from responsibility. On what terms would such a conversation take place? Did either man look the other in the eye?

This was not the whole extent of the ministry's miscalculations. They made three other expensive mistakes. By far the most costly – and most curious – had been to write into all their calculations of oil-company income an assumption that the profits made from the North Sea would carry the regular U.K. tax of more than 50 per cent. This overlooked the fact that any oil company registered in the U.K. could charge as a 'tax loss' against its profits all the royalties paid to other oil sources, mainly the Arabs. Since until then there had been no prospect of profits arising from U.K. wells, these 'tax losses' had accumulated, and were able to do so from year to year. And since the volume of oil on which royalties were paid elsewhere was far greater than the potential of the North Sea wells, and since the Arabs were raising their royalties, the 'tax losses' would be so vast as to more than cover future profits from the North Sea.

In fact, by 1971 the companies had accumulated £1,500m. in 'tax losses', running by then at an average of £350m. a year. With the worth of North Sea oil at its peak in 1980 estimated at £2,500m. a year, the companies were due for a 'tax holiday' for years. They also got from the British government huge capital-development and depreciation allowances to further soften the burden.

As early as 1964, when the fatal policy was being drawn up, the Inland Revenue department had warned the Petroleum Division: 'In discussion the companies and we have *tacitly accepted the fiction* [my italics] that all companies will pay U.K. tax at the full rate. In fact we know that the two largest British companies pay hardly any tax in this country at the present time because of double taxation and other reliefs.' This memorandum was conveniently buried and the 'fiction' presented to ministers as a token of the suffering to be endured by the noble oil companies as they hit oil.

The two other errors helped to convey a picture of Britain getting an equitable piece of the action. The ministry had said that, through British holdings in the oil companies, the direct benefit to the country was 21 per cent of the ownership of licensed territory. But this made the elementary mistake of assuming that Shell was a wholly British company; allowing for the fact that Britain had only 40 per cent meant that the national stake was not 21 per cent but 12 per cent. The same sloppy work produced 'evidence' that the British share of back-up services like pipelines and rigs was 50 per cent, again on an assumption that companies operating in Britain were British. In many cases large slices of the profits were remitted elsewhere, mostly to the U.S.A. The real British share was 25 per cent.

But Sir Robert Marshall was unrepentant. The true face of the Custodian never lost its composure. After all the 'fictions' and miscalculations were apparent, Sir Robert could only say: ' ... in one way or another the market would have supported some strengthening of the terms and we may have made a misjudgment there, but I do not think it was a very large misjudgment.'

In the auction, a consortium of Shell and Exxon had paid £20m. for one block. And they were not paying that kind of money simply on a hunch.

After the years of negligence, Heath's government did the only thing it could do. It undertook to tax the North Sea profits at the full rate. Davies was, with seeming decorum, moved from the Trade ministry to become Minister to Europe.

Had the oil-men been weeping crocodile tears? The perils of the North Sea were not exaggerated, but once the equipment was right the score of successful oil strikes was extraordinarily high: one wild-cat in every fifteen yielded a viable supply; in the U.S.A. only one in fifty proves profitable. Even at a cost of between £1m. and £2m. for opening a well, the North Sea is regarded as pay-dirt. In the British sector there are now nearly 250 separate commercial interests involved. But perhaps the final give-away comes from Sir Frank McFadzean, chairman of Shell in London. He admitted: 'Every calculation we have made on investing has been on the basis that we would pay corporate tax on every barrel we take from the North Sea. We have always anticipated that the government would do what it is going to do.'

In other words, the innocence of the Custodians had been too obvious to last. While it had, the oil-men took full advantage of it. They had never, for example, been asked or obliged to tell the ministry what their real costs were.

Through 1973 the rate of oil strikes in the northern sector of the British North Sea made the early pessimism evaporate. The bulk of the notorious fourth-round blocks were on the extreme north-eastern perimeter, including the highest-priced one of all, block 211/21 bought by Shell/

Exxon, which was between the Shetland Islands and Norway. For the languishing economy of Scotland, the oil rush was a new Klondike. For Britain the strikes held out the prospects of providing at least two-thirds, 150m. tons, of the country's oil needs by 1980. With the sudden escalation of Arab oil prices, the anxiety to press the exploration was proved right – but to achieve it the country surrendered far too much.

In 1973 the Petroleum Division of the D.T.I., its gifts dispensed, announced an increase in its staff of experts, from ten to twenty.

11

Nasty Tricks in the League of Gentlemen:
Giving capitalism a bad name

Before Edward Heath, no Tory Prime Minister, whatever
the provocation, had the nerve to bite the hand that fed the
party funds. So that when in the House of Commons Heath
described one company as 'the unpleasant and unacceptable
face of capitalism' it was an historic as well as a rhetorical
moment. As the man who had legitimized the Hustlers,
Heath needed to be careful about finding targets for his
abuse. In this case, he could hardly have kept silent.

As the British pulled out of Africa in the nineteen-
fifties and 'sixties they left unstable political situations and
nascent economies. For anyone with an eye for business
opportunities it was a risky but potentially lucrative field of
operation. British businessmen, used for so long to having
captive and monopolized markets, could no longer rely on
their imperial airs and graces – nor were they popular. But
the emergent countries badly needed technical expertise
and men who could build up their trade. Roland 'Tiny'
Rowland, well over six feet tall, was a man who saw this
chance and who happened to be equipped for it.

Rowland was born in India, the son of a German trader.
Because of this parentage he was put into detention in
Britain during World War II. After the war he drifted from
one fruitless job to another, and then emigrated to Rhodesia.
In the calm of the colonial twilight he prospered as a farmer.
In England the sallow skin of the 'Anglo-Indian' had
marked him out; in Rhodesia, amongst the tanned white
settlers, Rowland developed British upper-class manners
and accents in an almost exaggerated self-grooming. He
became a surrogate gentleman. But there was just enough

of the exotic about him, together with his indomitable charm, to avoid the harder, patrician edge that Africans disliked in the style of the whites. Without quite realizing it, Rowland had acquired the ideal characteristics for an entrepreneur in the new Africa.

Some time in 1960, Rowland met a young British businessman in Rhodesia, a man of impeccable connexions and a rising reputation as a shrewd dealer. The Honourable Angus Ogilvy was a director of a banking group which had invested in a company called the London and Rhodesian Mining Company, or Lonrho for short. Ogilvy was not happy with the way Lonrho was going, and decided after meeting Rowland that this beguiling man had just the kind of energy the company needed. In 1961 Ogilvy put Lonrho into Rowland's care. It was a happy inspiration, and a rapport grew rapidly between the two men. When Rowland joined Lonrho its net profits before tax were £158,000. By 1972 they were £19·3m. In that time Rowland had acquired 400 subsidiary companies. Lonrho's interests were spun intricately through both black and white Africa, and included railways, mining, car-dealerships and newspapers. In three of the new African states, Zambia, Zaïre and Ghana the political leaders regarded Rowland as almost a national asset.

The fact that Rowland's intimate colleague on the Lonrho board was Angus Ogilvy, husband of Princess Alexandra, a cousin of the Queen, did not hurt. The princess had helped out the Royal Family in the arduous chore of attending the ceremonials lowering the Union Jack for the last time in colonial outposts. She is paid £10,000 a year for her services.

Although on its record Lonrho seemed a model testimony to Rowland's talents, there were growing problems in its accounts. It was a London-based company, quoted on the London Stock Exchange, but most of its earnings came from Africa, and much of its profit was unremittable to London. At the end of 1971 the money flowing out from

London to finance new projects had outstripped the money coming in, and there was a cash crisis. Ogilvy commissioned a report into Lonrho's finances by accountants. This uncovered the consequences of Rowland's highly personal style of running the company. He had built the business on his own contacts – without Rowland there would have been no Lonrho. But Rowland had little patience with bureaucratic procedure or the boardroom consensus. He preferred to fly solo. This style was anathema to the conventional corporate accountants, and it cut corners on the codes of business practice, such as they were.

Although Ogilvy wanted a semblance of orthodoxy imposed on Lonrho he knew better than anybody that Rowland carried the company. He was not anxious to see Rowland's wings clipped. His solution was window-dressing. Lonrho would acquire some gentlemen.

It was a noble intention, but management by grey eminence was against Rowland's temperament. And one of the new Lonrho directors seemed to have been picked as the antithesis of everything that Rowland stood for. Sir Basil Smallpeice represented a kind of instant sobriety. He was highly esteemed by the City Establishment on grounds which seemed the essence of tradition: his personality had been determined by prudence. His arid pedantry had served him well as managing director of B.O.A.C., an airline run like a branch of the civil service. His later chairmanship of the shipping line Cunard had ended when that company fell victim to take-over. The Hustlers moved in and Smallpeice moved out. He was stripped along with the assets.

When Smallpeice took over as deputy chairman of Lonrho and began to get a sense of Rowland's cavalier style his demeanour, which normally suggested a man walking in fear of offensive odours, became acutely discomfited. Recoiling from an excursion into the company accounts, Smallpeice consulted other directors and emerged as the leader of a dissenting caucus. As the board became polarized between Rowland and the Smallpeice faction, another distinctly singular character popped up in the middle. Rowland had made his own move to recruit a figure of esteem, somebody who could both ingratiate Lonrho back into the City's favours and at the same time lubricate its African business. His choice was the Rt. Hon. Duncan Sandys, M.P.

The appearance of Sandys in the story, which was to become crucial, requires a digression to more illustrious adventures than the construction of an African business empire. Sandys represents a strange clique in British political life, as the survivor of a once elite band whose fortunes and reputation revealed the country's internal convulsions and external bravura.

A colleague of Sandys in a post-war Tory Cabinet called him one of those 'overgrown Boy Scouts'. This was a bit harsh. Sandys had behind him one of the most valuable and least acknowledged coups of World War II, the crippling of Wernher von Braun's V-2 rocket sites, which, according to Eisenhower, made the D-Day landings possible. When Sandys, in R.A.F. intelligence, detected the sites the top military brass reacted with scorn and disbelief. But Sandys had leverage. He was Churchill's son-in-law. The R.A.F. was ordered to blast the launching-pads.

Not only marriage tied Sandys to the Churchill clan. Before the war he had been an opponent of appeasement; after the war he encouraged Churchill into a theme of European unity. But on the way he contracted a fatal flaw, hyper-patriotism which curdled easily into imperial lament. At Suez Sandys was a gunboat diplomatist. As the colonies were shed he rushed around Africa trying to ensure that the new nations were respectful of British values. He lectured their leaders in the best Old Etonian manner. He loved telling the story of how he found President Kwame Nkrumah of Ghana cowering from public view because he feared assassination. Sandys insisted that Nkrumah take a ride through Accra in an open car and, for good measure, forced him out of the car and into the crowds. As Sandys described it, the moral was that True Brit could put back the spine into the most abject coward. When coloured immigration became an issue, Sandys was an early hard-line opponent.

With this kind of history, it might have seemed tactless of Rowland to recruit Sandys to the cause of maintaining Lonrho's good relations in black Africa, but Sandys was so thick-skinned that any suggestion of white paternalism amazed him. Moreover, he was politically versatile enough to have kept useful contacts in South Africa, where Lonrho was very active.

Without consulting the board, Rowland hired Sandys as a consultant at £50,000 a year. Three months later this was increased by £1,000 and the contract extended to six years. Of this money, £49,000 was to be paid into a tax haven in the Cayman Islands as an 'overseas fee'. But Rowland decided that he needed Sandys in a more visible role. The consultancy deal was scrapped and Sandys was appointed chairman at £40,000 a year. This apparent sacrifice was more than compensated for. Rowland paid Sandys £130,000 into the Cayman Islands as settlement for the loss of a consultancy that the Lonrho board didn't even know about until two weeks after they formally invited him to be chairman.

All this made Smallpeice apoplectic, but, for a while, Rowland had the continuing support of Ogilvy, his original sponsor. Sandys naturally backed Rowland, and so did another new representative of board-room prestige, Edward du Cann. Whereas Sandys represented the amputated Churchillian limb of the Tory party, Du Cann was a founder member of the Hustler's academy of the new capitalism. He was a former colleague of Peter Walker and a former chairman of the Tory party, though now a disaffected follower of Edward Heath. He arrived at Lonrho as chairman of the merchant bank Keyser, Ullman.

For a company with problems, Lonrho had attracted heavyweight support. This face of capitalism was well connected – with the Tory party, with the City, with the lingering aura of Churchill, and – by reflected glory via the Ogilvy connexion – with the Royal Family. Smallpeice himself had once served as comptroller at Buckingham Palace, charged with the task of introducing modern business methods to the household management, without conspicuous results.

It is axiomatic in the City Establishment's code that if dirt is about to fly the room should empty quickly before the innocent are contaminated. As the Smallpeice faction became rebellious, the Hon. Angus Ogilvy regretfully resigned from the board of Lonrho 'because of the situation that has arisen'. Lonrho's linen was about to be not just washed in public, but flaunted.

Smallpeice, who gave the impression that he would rather have lost his shirt than his probity, led eight Lonrho directors who wanted Rowland sacked. To stop them Rowland applied for an injunction in the High Court. This meant that for several days an incredulous nation was treated to a recital of charge and counter-charge which disclosed intrigue, high-living and rapacity and was accompanied by the sound of collapsing reputations. Nothing quite like it had ever come from the mouths of gentlemen in public.

An important part of Smallpeice's case concerned complex and cloudy dealings in Africa, some involving the Ogilvy family trusts. But it was not these that caught the public attention. Rowland's grand style of living, including a £350,000 country mansion donated free by the company, triggered off a wail of Puritan horror. So too did the details of Rowland's open-handed treatment of Sandys, especially the use of the tax haven.

Although Sandys immediately declared that £44,000, handed over as the first instalment of his 'compensation', destined for the Cayman Islands, had been paid back to Lonrho, these dealings made Sandys as much as Rowland a lightning-conductor for public outrage. Sandys' response, totally in character, was to clench his simian jaw even more tightly and say that the attacks on Rowland 'were mostly of a very vague nature'. Rowland had good cause to reflect that if you wanted a man to go into the jungle with you, Duncan Sandys was a good choice.

The High Court ruled in favour of Smallpeice, but had to yield the final constitutional sanction to the Lonrho shareholders. 'Whichever way the voting goes', said the chairman of a body called the Wider Share Ownership Council, 'this is shareholder democracy in action.' The shareholders voted six-to-one to keep Rowland and dump Smallpeice and his supporters.

On the face of it, the cavalier had been vindicated against the puritan. The sentiment of the shareholders, at least the hundreds of them who turned up for the public vote, was clearly that Rowland was a man who made empires and that Smallpeice was a man who filled ledgers. (Rowland complained that during his tenure at Lonrho Smallpeice never once visited any of the African operations.) The assembled shareholders seemed predominantly *petit bourgeois*, from the massed ranks of the Tory grassroots. They were un-impressed by appeals that tax havens and company mansions were immoral. They probably sensed, correctly, the cant in such a charge. The British shires are dotted with houses, cars, farms, racing stables and boats that are funded by companies. Gentlemen regarded these as the legitimate fruits of capitalism. As for screwing the tax-man, well, everybody was in favour of that. One shareholder explained: 'Tiny is a latter-day saint of capitalism, the sort of man to whom the small shareholder will entrust his life savings.'

Exit Smallpeice, seeking calmer waters.

Not only Sandys, du Cann and the shareholders had backed up Rowland; several of the black African leaders intimated that if he were to disappear they would take a very poor view of it. They certainly didn't share Harold Wilson's predictable description of Lonrho as 'a fetid swamp in the Tory free-for-all jungle'.

For Heath the Lonrho affair had been uncomfortable.

His definition of the 'unpleasant and unacceptable face of capitalism' had been impulsive, but it reflected a revulsion that was apolitical. The roles of Sandys and Du Cann stung him personally. Du Cann was chairman of a powerful pressure group of Tory M.P.s, and he made a point of being evangelistic about his work in establishing, with Walker, wider share-ownership through unit trusts. It was all uncomfortably close to the 'New Capitalism'; only Rowland's flamboyance marked out his career from the more bloodless calculations of the Slater, Walker history.

It is understandable that Heath should have been ambivalent about big business. On one hand he was its most committed supporter; on the other he was continually provoked into anger by dilatory managements which put self-interest before the national interest. Heath was like a man doing social work amongst the whores in the hope of redeeming them; each time one of them lifted her skirts in public the embarrassment was acute. The Lonrho affair was a microcosm of all the social, political and commercial attitudes fogging the path of reformers. As such, it seemed a good deal more real than any of the pious appeals to the public spirit.

12

Cultural defoliation:
Kissing goodbye to Piccadilly

Even the most casual visitor to London cannot help but notice that Piccadilly Circus is a semi-derelict slum. Superficially it seems a victim of urban blight. Seedy porno shops, skin movies, pinball arcades and cheap hamburger joints are all around it. In the centre, once supposed to be the heart both of the empire and of the world, the island bearing Eros has been chopped away for the convenience of traffic. Behind neon façades the buildings are flaking and unkempt. But this has not been caused by the attrition of urban nihilism. Piccadilly Circus is a pawn in an elaborate game which has made a few men rich and at the same time eaten away the historic roots of London more insidiously than any cancer.

London is not the only capital to fall under the rapacity of the property speculator. But the difference between London and most other victims is that each time a building is demolished an irreplaceable piece of history is likely to go with it. Not only is London extremely vulnerable to this kind of cultural defoliation, but it is also the home and training-ground of a band of men who have set out to raze other cities across the world. One of True Brit's successful exports is a highly sophisticated technique for turning destruction into gold.

London lacks the martial perspectives of Paris, the baroque chaos of Rome. It's an unplanned city, assembled piecemeal with history piled up like silt along its streets. Modern London still follows the street plan of Stuart London. Until this century that plan determined the city's perspectives and scale; the texture was all of a piece. Without the imposition of a grand design, London was coherent. In a thousand years a city rich in character had been built.

After Hitler's demolition work the first wave of reconstruction, from the late 'forties to the mid 'fifties, exposed the bankruptcy of modern British architecture. The crime was aesthetic, not venal. The second wave, from the late 'fifties to the mid 'sixties, was different. The demand was for offices, and it transformed cubic blocks of air-space into fortunes for developers, who were allowed to bulldoze away priceless historic buildings. But there was a third assault, and this marked a kind of new maths which did for property development what asset-stripping did simultaneously to industry. It transformed nominal values into astronomical ones.

A relatively small group of people devised and played this game. There are three steps in it. The first is to identify the most valuable sites, and then to acquire them with such stealth that the people selling the separate parts are kept ignorant of their real value. The second is to negotiate with planning authorities a scheme to maximize the rentable space. Having thus assembled not just a building but a machine capable virtually of printing money, the final step is what might be called Chinese book-keeping: borrowing the finance for construction with the planning permission as sufficient collateral, then capitalizing the scheme on its realizable income. It is an ingenious technique involving a marginal outlay, no risk, and stupendous profits. There were peculiar reasons why it worked in London better than anywhere else.

Office space was already at a premium in the early 'sixties, but the Labour government, in one of its most counter-productive strokes, turned a good thing into a bonanza. They slapped a ceiling on office developments which, after a deadline, depended on getting tightly limited permits. With the supply curtailed, the rent per square foot in central London went from £2·25 a square foot in 1965 to £6 in 1970. Although the restraints were then modified the escalation continued. By 1973 prime space in the City of London was nearly £20 a square foot – five times the current price in Manhattan. The capital value of an office block is put at twenty times the annual rent it produces. For one London scheme alone this meant a capital value of at least £200m. on construction costs of £46m.

With pickings of this size, a juggernaut was unleashed. Property development in central London bore no relation to social need, and carried no mercy for the city's vulnerable historical fabric. The city's legislators and administrators, the only people with the power to contain and control re-development, were babes in arms when confronted by the guile and blandishments of the speculators. Planning officers were conned into surrendering key sites in return for peanuts – tower blocks seemed to do something for their ego. The city was being robbed, by consent.

The memorial to this philosophy and age is the 34-storey office tower Centre Point, which dominates the skyline of London's West End. It was built in 1964, but stayed empty for ten years. Not because it was a lemon, but because it was worth more empty than full. The man who built it, Harry Hyams, was simply waiting for the market to meet his price – £1m. a year. Until it did, 202,000 square feet of space appreciating year by year, Hyams could afford to wait. The London boom had made him a personal fortune of over £300m.

Stung by Hyams's brass nerve, Peter Walker saw Centre Point as a blemish on his New Capitalism. In September 1972 he told Parliament: 'The time has come to bring an end to this highly undesirable practice.' Hyams's response was to advertise the building in European newspapers as 'the best-known office building in the world'. But notoriety was not enough. There were still no takers. And Peter Walker could huff and puff but he couldn't blow Centre Point down. Built for £4m., this memorial to inflation was now worth £40m.

The struggle between property speculators and local

authorities is an unequal one. In other countries the conjunction of such an opportunity for vast personal gain and the relatively modest means of the men dispensing the licence to make that gain would create the perfect conditions for graft. It can also work out that way in Britain. But naivety is in some ways more of a vice than corruption. The smart property speculator in London might say with some truth: 'When things go so well without corruption, why introduce it?'

Property speculation in London brings into play, on the one side, planning officers (many not even trained planners) earning about £3,000 a year, and on the other side a number of men wearing camel-hair coats who run Rolls-Royces with television in the rear seats and who can pick up a clear £400,000 or more a year. The planning officer has little commercial sophistication. He is probably highly scrupulous, a pedant on planning laws, and socially very impressionable. The result is not corruption. It is the intercourse, familiar in Britain, of the amateur and the professional.

It is Piccadilly Circus, that hub of the universe, that shows what happens when the jackals group in the undergrowth around a promising carcass. From 1959 the Circus was a battleground for the competing fashions of urban planning and architecture. The first developer to see its potential for self-enrichment was Jack Cotton, the man who dropped the Pan Am building across Park Avenue to block out the sky. Cotton's plans were undermined by a counter-attack by aesthetes, not by popular sentiment. A succession of alternatives, each reflecting the fads of their time, were proposed for the Circus: bigger roads; 'piazzas'; overhead pedestrian 'walkways'; neon-girdled 'entertainment complexes'.

By 1965 speculators had quietly prospected and bought up the three major blocks available for redevelopment on the fringe of the Circus. The fancier ideas had given way to hard commercial logic. One plan included 544,000 square feet of office space calculated to make a profit of £27·5m. This was the brainchild of Joe Levy, one of the founding fathers of the London boom. Levy's plan was so flagrant that the legislators acceded to public uproar and promised, at least, to limit the height of the new buildings to the old. But people like Levy and Hyams don't take kindly to having their wings clipped. If the legislators didn't go along with him, Levy warned, 'you can all kiss goodbye to a new Piccadilly Circus'.

Although the name of the game was exposed in Piccadilly, its ultimate scope was understood by very few Londoners. Demolition and redevelopment are dispersed and involve a time-lapse. The dimensions of the London defoliation are staggering both in what has already been done and what will be done. In the City of London alone, where the layers of history are at their deepest, 130 major sites went ahead simultaneously. More than a quarter of the City's archeological deposits have been destroyed by the digging of deep basements. There is no legal requirement to consider archaeological value before development. The work of centuries in which buildings were shaped to the needs of people is being interred by the needs of the fast buck. Less than a fifth of the material evidence for Roman, Saxon and mediaeval London survives; in twenty years it will have gone.

In the London that in little more than a decade created a new crop of multi-millionaires, a quarter of the housing stock is structurally condemned. In the inner belt two-thirds of the homes were built before the end of World War I, most of them between 1875 and 1919. These are not buildings which merit preservation other than as examples of the squalor which was socially acceptable to Victorians and Edwardians. There are 250,000 houses lacking basic facilities like indoor sanitation. Legislators bemused by the 'prestige' of office blocks and hungry for the taxes they generate have been cynically tardy in sweeping away these slums.

The ten largest property companies in 1973 controlled assets of about £3,000m. – more than the entire gold and dollar reserves of the country. Joe Levy, like Harry Hyams, had made a vast personal fortune by 1972, and was still not acting like a satisfied man. Hyams's architect, a former army officer called Colonel Richard Seifert, has had more influence on the London skyline than Wren, but with rather less distinction. Still, his company has a turnover of more than £50m. a year.

But London will not be the sole beneficiary of British developers and speculators. By 1973 British firms had £750m.-worth of office blocks under way in Europe. In Brussels alone there were thirty-five towers to commemorate British enterprise. In Paris a British developer, having made a killing among the innocent there by using the London Method, predicted that they would have to ease up. The natives were rising. Even in New York, following the early precedent of the Pan Am building, British developers sniffed opportunity. The old country still had one or two kinds of colonialism left to play.

Six hundred and fifty miles north of London you come to the end of the British Isles, at the island of Unst. This is one of the Shetland Islands, with a hundred miles of sea between them and the northern tip of Scotland. Around the serrated shoreline of Unst the Atlantic meets the North Sea. It is farther north than Leningrad, and on the same latitude as Anchorage, Alaska. But thanks to the Gulf Stream Unst is frost-free in the winter. Despite this, no trees grow on Unst and the winds cut through anything but stone. The place-names are a blend of Celtic and Nordic: Uyeasound, Mu Ness, Muckle Flugga, and Baltasound.

This is the land of the Norsemen. A Scandinavian king traded the Shetlands to Scotland in 1468, and by the devolutions of warfare the Shetlanders ended up being called British. But nothing farther from the urban refinements of London is imaginable. Until the 1970s the 800 inhabitants of Unst were self-sustaining and independent; there was no unemployment, and the only problem was a trickling wastage of the younger people to the city lights a few hundred miles and a world away to the south. Twentieth-century blights passed Unst by. The only callers were mainly fishermen: Norwegians, Danes, Faroese and Ice-landers running for shelter from storms into Unst's tiny harbour of Norwick. The island's one bar was apt to see its whisky reserves vanish overnight.

For people at peace with the world and needing none of its more contrived pleasures, Unst was as near Utopian as the spirit could crave. Then came the oil-men. The two basins running to the east and west of the Shetlands are probably the richest oil deposits of the new bonanza. The cloud over the composure of the Shetlands is affluence. An early estimate of what the oil business could be worth to the Shetlands was £10m. a year. From a condition of thrifty contentment the 17,000 Shetlanders have the prospect of becoming one of Britain's richest communities. But there is a price to be paid.

Of the three main Shetland Islands, Unst is the least impressed by the prospects of a fortune from oil. Its tradi-tional sources of income, fishing and crofting, are tough but automatically self-selecting. Nobody works like that unless they enjoy it. Fish-processing is the Shetlands' main industry, but on Unst this smacks too much of organized activity. Fishing, crofting, and breeding Shetland ponies are closer to God. Supporting the needs of oil companies is something else. But elsewhere in the Shetlands people are less immune to temptation. Even the smallest bureaucracy becomes devious when financial gain is put into jeopardy by the normal democratic processes.

Four oil companies, Shell, Exxon, British Petroleum, and Conoco, coveted the Shetlands as the nearest landfall to their new wells. They wanted new harbours, storage tanks, and a refinery. The refinery would be one of the biggest in Europe: 650 acres. It would be run with a staff of 600, and would need 5,000 imported workmen to build it. The total Shetlands labour force is only 3,000.

A 33-strong County Council governs the Shetlands. Within the council a committee in control of planning swiftly became a pro-oil lobby. In six months the price of land around the Shetland capital of Lerwick rose from £1,000 an acre to £4,000 an acre, and kept rising. There was only one problem in the path of this boom: people. In places like Baltasound on Unst, selected as a site for a harbour and storage depot, those living the simple life of honest labour were in the way. In one croft, for example, a young widow scratched out a meagre living with poultry and vegetables, but still felt disinclined to move aside for the bulldozer. Others also resisted, aware of the 'modifications' of the landscape proposed to accommodate the oil industry. The reluctant widow and her allies were regarded by the council's oil caucus as short-sighted and obstructionist – the kind of epithets used by zealous administrators the world over. Bureaucrats impeded in this way turn their mind to law, and if the law is uncooperative they turn their mind to making new law.

The sixteen Shetlanders inside the oil caucus decided to set up a Port and Harbour Authority. It would be empowered by law to remove people in the path of progress. It would be able to compulsorily purchase the holdings of stubborn widows, giving only twenty-eight days' notice before the bulldozers moved in. The price paid would be at the Authority's discretion. The 'master plan' for the Authority was drawn up by consulting engineers in London at a cost of £70,000. Nobody on the Shetland Islands but the members of the oil lobby saw these plans, although the oil companies were consulted. The politics of the Shetlands, until then placidly parochial, began to show all the signs of cosmopolitan intrigue. They attracted the energies of oilmen, consulting engineers, developers, and numerous parasites who, at the first whiff of oil in the nostrils, flock to the scene. Men measured the price of other men.

Once every two weeks the bank arrives on Unst, weather permitting. The bank is a man with a suitcase full of notes from the five Scottish banks. Money has so far played a modest part in that spartan life. But the oil is coming.

Environmentalism, that slovenly word, is a fashion. The barbarism it faces is a tradition. Beautiful buildings have been thoughtlessly destroyed by each generation's needs and sense of its own superiority. The British invented the Industrial Revolution, and they have been as mindless as anyone of its by-products. Industrial pollution began in the Elysian dales of Derbyshire. The heart of England was clawed out to feed the furnace of Mammon. As the innovator, Britain now has the world's worst legacy of industrial wreckage: deposits of burned-out industries, ravaged land, and exhausted people.

More than a quarter of a million acres of land in England and Wales is classified as 'derelict'. This is really a euphemism: it is dead land, consumed and discarded, barren and toxic. It can offer life to nothing else. And these vast wastes do not include industrial slums: in 1973 there were still two-and-a-half million people in England and Wales living in houses classified by the euphemism of 'unfit', lacking one or all of the basic amenities of hot water, bath or indoor lavatory. In many cities the conditions are getting worse, not better.

The most neglected areas are the seedbeds of industrialism. In the north of England 16 per cent of the homes have outside lavatories, compared to 7 per cent in the south-east. The worst conditions are in Scotland, where things have been so bad for so long that the population is draining south. In Glasgow, a city without a centre or a soul, the population has shrunk from 1·2 million in 1945 to 900,000 in 1972, and is falling at the rate of 25,000 a year.

The worst pollution and the worst housing coincide, afflicting the most defenceless and poorest people: the working class marooned in the discarded debris of the nineteenth-century industrial baronies. New 'clean' industries and their white-collar workers are outside the dying cities. The two unhealthiest regions, measured by the incidence of deaths from lung cancer, heart disease and bronchitis, are north-west England and Scotland – the places containing the most abject slums. The highest levels of lead contamination in the blood of children are in the urban working-class neighbourhoods.

This human and physical degradation ought to be the most sobering restraint on the pouring of public funds into new airports and the channel tunnel. But when social remedy and commercial interests compete the real priorities of True Brit become clear. Official 'policy' reveals the dichotomy. The Department of the Environment is little better than a cynical exercise in tokenism. The Department of Trade and Industry, with totally opposing interests and values, has the upper hand. The conflict was exquisitely embodied in one man: Peter Walker.

Walker was the first Environment Minister – the first in the world, as he pointed out to an international conference of conservationists. The Ministry is, in truth, a sham piece of window-dressing covering the convenience of a bureau-cratic merger of transport, planning, and local-government administration. Walker found no conflict in moving across to head the D.T.I.: one day the gamekeeper, the next the poacher. He showed the same agility in business. While the Environment Ministry neglects the slums, the D.T.I. spon-sors a new phase of industrial rape. They are funding with £50m. the commercial exploration of British mineral deposits.

This is not just a generous subsidy to already rich com-panies (Rio Tinto Zinc, an immediate beneficiary, made profits of £119m. in 1973) in the form of a 35 per cent chunk of exploration costs. It is a frontal assault on a treasured national asset. The remaining minerals of any worth are mostly in the National Parks. Less than £1m. a year is spent on maintaining the Parks; with the government subsidy about £100m. is being spent on mineral exploration. By the 1980s it is estimated that £100m.-worth of non-ferrous metal can be mined in Britain, a sixth of the country's imports. The bulk of this would have to come from the National Parks. An open-cast mine for non-ferrous metals covers 1,500 acres and needs 3,000 more acres for surrounding activity. The metals are some of the most poisonous to man, animals and plants.

Peter Walker talked of 'a new age of elegance for the mass of the people', about as meaningful as his 'New Capitalism' was for the people. As a policing agent, the Environment Ministry is a fraud. The housing department was caught trying to cover its bad record by 'fixing' Parliamentary questions in its favour; the transport department has a reputation for excessive secrecy and for ruthlessly overriding environmental objections to road plans. One of Walker's first acts was to announce 1,000 miles of new motorways.

The sceptred isle, set in a silver sea, is being systematically poisoned. The sea and the rivers are employed as the rectum of industry. A survey of thirty-two British coastal resorts shows that thirty-one of them discharge their sewage into the sea. In rivers, 60 per cent of the sewage and 50 per cent of the effluents are discharged illegally. In 1971 the average fine for oil spillage from tankers was £200. In spite of tougher legislation, ninety convictions in one year totalled only £22,125 in fines. For industrial pollution the penalties have become more frequent. In half a century there were three prosecutions. Since 1967 there have been two a year. The fines are £100 a time.

13 *A land fit for fiddlers:*
The boom in backhanders

The pretence of moral superiority sustains True Brit as much as anything. To concede the same flaws of character that so regrettably afflict other so-called advanced industrial states would be one more erosion of the hubris which allows the British to walk tall. It would also be one step nearer to reality. Anybody unlucky enough to be caught downwind of the thalidomide case, the Hustlers, Lonrho, or the property developers might be forgiven for wondering what 'playing the game' really means. Games were being played all right, but by what rules, and in whose interest?

They might all, of course, be random aberrations and lacking in profound significance. That is one view, and True Brit would like you to share it. Or you can take the partisan line. Harold Wilson always does, though nobody has more convenient amnesia than he. For a few years takeovers and mergers were 'industrial rationalization', and then suddenly they were rampant capitalism. And it was George Brown's restrictions on new office-building in London that created the most rapacious phase of property speculation.

But sanctimonious indignation was not confined to the Labour party. The scrap between Tiny Rowland and Basil Smallpeice forced Edward Heath on to very thin ice with his 'unacceptable face of capitalism' disclaimer, made the more tenuous by his own closeness to the Hustlers. Heath certainly had a bad run: Reginald Maudling, his Deputy Prime Minister, left suddenly under a cloud. There were continual embarrassments from the City, where whatever the tokens of reform, the major activity remained the making of the fast buck rather than the less self-serving activity of financing industrial renewal. British companies were caught paying starvation wages in South Africa, and Mr William Luke, chairman of the United Kingdom South Africa Trading Association, in 1973 blithely told a committee of enquiring M.P.s: 'There is a tendency for the African, if you pay him more money, to put in less time' – higher wages shouldn't be paid, he said, for 'incompetent labour'. There was the case of Sir Denys Lowson buying shares valued at £474,000 and a few months later making a profit on them of £5m. (though after this was disclosed he agreed to hand back the profit). And there was the second-mortgage scandal in which the customers unwittingly paid up to 25 per cent interest.

To explain away these things in ideological terms, either as endemic to a Tory regime or – as Heath attempted – as warts rather than infections, misses the point. What made them distinctive was their visibility rather than their rarity. It was the difference between an assumed set of ethical values and actual behaviour. The tradition of 'confidentiality', so essential to the *mores* of the club, was not always holding fast. At one time for a company to have crucified itself in public, as Lonrho had done, would have been unthinkable: it would all have been hushed up. But some businesses had acquired an obsessiveness which made them less discreet. Admittedly, these were only hairline cracks: the core of the clubs held to the old codes. The Hustlers could still be cold-shouldered; the compact of industrial and administrative power was secure. It was still credible to claim that the basic institutions retained their integrity.

And yet there is one substantial new source of disillusionment which seems a token of real ethical slipping: local government. The reluctance in Britain to accept the obvious about local government was based on a mixture of apathy and innocence; 60 or 70 per cent of the electorate don't even bother to vote in local elections. Perhaps because grassroots politics is right under everybody's nose it tends to be the least visible and the least interesting branch of government.

But the aura of the pedestrian, the prosaic and the boring is very misleading. Local government is now an adjunct of big business: it accounts for 16 per cent of the gross national product.

It was always fertile ground for corruption, though it was once mostly petty and frequently pathetic. Herbert Morrison, the first and most powerful of British city bosses, discovered extensive small-time fiddling when he entered London politics before World War I. Particularly in the East End, corruption provided desperately needed subsidies to the marginal lives of local politicians, and it was – until Morrison – accepted with fatalism. Morrison's own purging impulse was merciless. He said: 'The only thing for which I would preserve capital punishment would be jobbery, bribery and corruption in the public services or robbery from public funds.'

Local government provides the perfect nexus for corruption, the meeting ground of the tempter and the tempted. Elected councillors and paid officials both dispense substantial patronage. In numerous cases the patrons are also potentially beneficiaries of the patronage, as one property developer explains: 'There are far too many estate agents and builders who get themselves elected to local authorities and go on to planning committees.'

As well as providing the honey-pot, local government in Britain is really a microcosm of a section of *poujadiste* society and a mirror of that society's ethic. Outwardly scrupulous and modest, inwardly it seethes with ego and ambitions, commercial and political. Again, this society works through the system of the club, and in this case a series of interleaved clubs. There are discreet chains of personal contact and brotherhoods of interdependent business interests. The efficacy of such a network cannot be underrated, though it is intended to be. There are obvious parallels, none of them quite adequate: the Mafia is one, but it is much too flamboyant. Another is Freemasonry; but no formal system like that, with its adolescent rituals and elaborate ranking, even though covert, is subtle enough or pervasive enough for this purpose. Freemasonry is, if anything, *too* exclusive. Fiddling is an extensive and relentless activity, as one victim of the system explained in a letter to *The Times*:

> In my own experience, the organizing of minor building work – especially where planning permission and/or an improvement grant is concerned, and the word 'discretion' is involved, is susceptible to a local authority's whims, with corruption difficult to prove but with the authority, for example, imposing a builder of its own choice upon the unwilling householder – with the latter paying substantially more for the work than if he had been able to employ a builder of his own selection.

The very choice of the word 'fiddling' implies permissiveness – something bent but too petty to be really regarded as criminal, the little bit of rope that anybody should be allowed. During the austere late 'forties it was black-market dealing in luxuries, whisky, bananas, meat, and the dispensation of holidays in Margate that represented fiddling at its most organized and yet tolerated level. Tolerated, that is, except for an occasional and hypocritical essay in finding scapegoats like poor John Belcher, who was toppled by the minimal charities of Sidney Stanley. At a lower level fiddling was, and is, endemic in all the dodges that cheat customers and employers alike: catering fiddles are the easiest and most obvious ones. The seventy-five Royal Navy officers and ratings who were convicted of embezzling catering funds showed how easily small-time rackets can, with the help of a military operation, become a multi-million pound business.

In one sense fiddling of this kind is like a built-in corrective to economic inequity. People who don't think that they are paid well enough put their hand in the till when they can. In Britain the cynical acceptance of such devices springs from a belief that inequity is institutionalized and inescapable, part of the warfare of 'them and us', and that the only redress is to cheat.

In local government the rewards of cheating have been transformed. During the 'sixties and 'seventies new public building programmes pumped hundreds of millions through the hands of modestly rewarded councillors and officials. They built schools, hospitals, colleges, swimming pools, shopping centres, pithead baths, council-housing estates, and blocks of flats. At the least, as in some of the London boroughs chosen for office development, there was a great deal of gullibility. At the worst – and more widely than perhaps we shall ever know – fiddling came of age.

There are more than 30,000 elected members of local authorities (although on County Councils more than half of the seats are unopposed) and about 4,000 planners working in local government. Cultural, regional and even party traits influence the style and degree of fiddling. In some parts of the country with an unshakeable Socialist allegiance, at the grassroots level there is virtually a political sub-state run by the Labour party, tightly knit and federalized. Like Richard Daley's Chicago Democratic party machine, the network throughout local government is self-perpetuating and a law unto itself. The party caucuses are oligarchic, and the fief of committed men. To anybody lacking that kind of political conviction and without a taste for power on a local level it might seem dull and thankless work. Many councillors are manual workers or shopkeepers, as close to the soul of the Labour movement as you can get. The only time the party leaders so much as brush with this world is on an annual ceremonial visit, and the epicurean sheen of a Westminster-fed face still stands out in awkward relief in those bleak settings. But venality pulses away in the local party men, occasionally surfacing in a public catastrophe.

Before he was given a thirty-month sentence for taking £6,700 in backhanders, the ex-Mayor of one Yorkshire town gave from the dock a glimpse of the ignominy of fiddling as it had come to him:

> I had lost a job. I had to sell my house and go and live in a demolition area in conditions I had never lived in before where you have to walk three doors down the street to go to the toilet. I was meeting the police regularly. I was on the dole for the first time in my life. I had a number of problems and I was indeed under the weather with my health.'

Better-connected miscreants had softer cushions to fall back on; in the lusher pastures of the south and at the golf-club level the masons took care of their own, even the fallen. And at the highest level, even if the compromising act was no worse than unwariness, there was no question of sudden decrepitude. The clubs close ranks and take care of their own.

What has changed the style of fiddling as much as its new profit potential is the art, craft or arcane calling of public relations. The usual business hospitalities and incentives of wining, dining, and perks are impossible to regulate. The laws governing local-government transactions, so far as they exist, expect a court to be able to distinguish where generosity ends and influence begins. It is a daunting judgment to attempt, and one that the lubricant of public relations helps to obscure.

It is the P.R. men who provide the entertainment and set up the climate for an exercise in fiddling. What begins as an innocent excursion into free-loading easily ends in a nod and a wink, the ethics blurred by unaccustomed hedonism. A minor party hack who may have laboured impeccably for twenty years with no material benefit, in a lowly paid job and worrying about his health and a meagre pension, suddenly finds himself in command of tempting patronage and feels the complicity of the system. For him to resist the blandishments and proffered comforts requires the asceticism of a saint. The P.R. man pours him another glass of brandy and spells out the game. As with the politicians, so also with minor-league civil servants.

Men's prices are fixed, titles like 'consultant' and 'public-relations adviser' are allocated as the veneer to cover the rot. Sometimes the devices are ludicrously clumsy, smacking of the melodrama of Gordon Liddy and the Watergate Cubans. In one case a backhander of £800 in £1 notes was put into a brown-paper parcel, sealed with red wax, and left openly on the table during a Conservative Club lunch, to be taken away afterwards by somebody other than the man who had brought it.

Significantly, a lot more energy is applied to maintaining the fiction of incorruptibility than to devising and applying remedies. Mr Clifford Sellick, chairman of the Local Government Information Office, says: 'Evidence of a significant amount of corruption is just not there.' His proposed way of making this statement plausible is to appoint a public-relations officer to every county and district large enough to support his salary. Less given to euphoria, the journal *Municipal Engineering* has said that corruption in local government is unmeasured and unmeasurable because 'the really clever ones' are not caught. It's already beyond argument that the minority of not-so-clever ones who do get caught (and who are certainly measurable) represent something numerous enough to be serious. But the tardy response to calls for tighter regulations reveals the instinctive laxity of the codes of True Brit.

It had been left to councillors to voluntarily declare a conflict of interest whenever it was likely to arise; needless to say many of them were less than ardent in doing so. Some councils do now require their members to register their interests, but many councils vigorously resist even this basic step. When a similar measure was proposed for M.P.s a Labour Party working-group made the astonishing proposal that although a register should be compiled it ought to be kept 'in conditions of security' by the Speaker. The Labour Party, uncomfortably close to corruption at the grassroots, inclines more to the covert than the Conservatives, who did at least concede that the register should be open to inspection, although they regarded compulsion to file the information as too onerous, and left vague the definition of 'interests'.

There are more than fifty M.P.s with known connexions in public relations and advertising, four-fifths of them Tories, but there are more of them with undeclared links with commercial and political pressure-groups like the egregious Aims of Industry. It is far too late in the day to raise eyebrows over the corruption of language by the P.R.-washed minds in politics. Edward Heath, whose feeling for words has the grace of an old boot, has to retain an ad-man to write his most considered sermons. And if anyone has robbed language of its meaning, Harold Wilson bequeathed a glossary of political hyperbole. This is not a minor vice. Once verbal corruption is accepted, it is a relatively short step to the more insidious corruptions in which the P.R. ethic oils the path of contracts and causes.

It is wrong to see the brotherhood of the fiddlers as simply an uncouth activity of the lower orders. Amongst even Simon Pure civil servants at the highest level it is common for them to move, after a discreet pause, from public service into industrial posts where their ministry knowledge and contacts are their main asset. Inside such an essentially loose system the licence is wide. It is abetted by the adherence to secrecy on spurious pretexts; the misplaced faith in self-regulation; the assumption of a unique national rectitude; the preference for underpaid amateurs rather than adequately rewarded professionals.

Those who set out in the first place to exploit this system know how by preference and custom they will find plenty of discretion. If there is one thing the British dislike more than the suggestion that they are corrupt it is the energetic exposure of corruption. Each successive exposure of fiddling adds to the impression of a country which professes a belief in one set of values while ardently pursuing another: a human frailty, perhaps, and by no means peculiar to the British. But the British aren't really like that, are they? If they are ... well, *who* is there left?

Part Three

Super-Brit, Ultra Brit,
and attendant follies

14 Super-Brit:
The poisoning of patriotism

'*The recognized reality of patriotism is not mere citizenship ... it is for better for worse, for richer for poorer, in sickness and in health, in national growth and glory and in national disgrace and decline ... it is not to travel in the ship of state as a passenger but if need be to go down with the ship.*'
– G. K. CHESTERTON

Somewhere in those fluvial bloodbaths where Angles mingled with Saxons and gave a name to a mongrel race there is supposed to be a spring of racial purity. Nobody can quite place it. There is no shrine to mark it, no Mount of Olives. The mists of folk-lore obligingly obscure it. Perhaps it is not a time or a place at all, but something felt in the bones, the seed of True Brit passed in the genes from one generation to another. Its siren is patriotism.

Sooner or later every would-be regenerator of British greatness falls back on appeals to patriotism, and it is usually a sign that things are bad. Pretension must end in reality; in Britain nothing postpones reality like an appeal to patriotism. Nobody thought it absurd that Harold Wilson, the token realist, should equate industrial revival with colonial piracy. It was done in the name of patriotism. Likewise, Edward Heath rationalized his own obsession with megatheria by seeing it as some kind of virility test. Patriotism is tangled with greatness, and greatness is tangled with ego. To defy this concept of greatness is to be unpatriotic, and to be unpatriotic is the ultimate crime in the eyes of True Brit. Whether it is the Hustler posing as the good patriot, or the bankrupting of the treasury by trying to sustain a mythical value of sterling, or the pouring of public funds into 'prestige' projects, the most suspect motives can be made plausible by draping them in a Union Jack.

But patriotism used in this way is a kind of incipient alcoholism. A little nip now and again to warm the belly does no harm, but it easily becomes addictive. It takes increasingly large doses to sustain euphoria. In some men True Brit has now reached this desperate stage; they represent a poisoning of patriotism. As their appeals to patriotism become more extreme, they become increasingly intolerant of challenge. They know that in no other country can the 'national interest' be invoked on more specious grounds, and in no other country will it be so mutely respected. The mildest sceptic is, in their eyes, a traitor. Patriotism in this form, Super-Brit, serves as a repressive cover for anything from ministerial miscalculations (don't 'knock Britain') to deliberate deception. Patriotism has come to represent what the British *want* to see, rather than what is actually there.

Super-Brit is much like religious fanaticism: extremity of view born of a high sense of rectitude. The state takes the place of God, and if the state is Britain the divinity is far from being rational.

Portrait of a Patriot : 1
'Seek not to inquire for whom the bell tolls'
Quintin McGarel Hogg, the second Lord Hailsham, is a muscular Christian. Fashions in political doctrine do not move him; if he has any recognizable and consistent strand of political faith it is patriotism. Until 1970 he was regarded as a distinguished lawyer who had sublimated a legal career for a political one. But he had served the Tory party long and faithfully without satisfying either his own innermost ambitions or other people's early expectations. Then, just when he seemed over the hill, Edward Heath appointed him Lord Chancellor. It was a considerable consolation prize. Nobody more dissimilar to the new Tory philistines could be imagined than Hailsham, with his button-up boots,

bicycle-riding and fiery revivalist rhetoric.

Twice Hailsham had been frozen out of the Tory party's higher councils; once by Churchill after he had attacked the great man's post-war policies, and again – more cruelly – by Macmillan, who gave him the derisory post of Minister of Science.

The complexity of Hailsham's Super-Brit showed at the time of Suez. As First Lord of the Admiralty under Eden he was – like that other hyper-patriot Duncan Sandys – well in the Bulldog Drummond camp, keen to give the wogs a biffing. None the less he was sensitive enough to discourage the shelling of Alexandria. But after the invasion was stopped, the United Nations enraged Hailsham by rejecting the help of the Royal Navy in clearing sunken hulks from the Suez Canal – it was a slight to British skills and pride.

When Macmillan succeeded Eden it was Hailsham, as party chairman, who rallied the shattered spirits so effectively that – against all the predictions – Macmillan won the next election. But it was while he was helping this resurrection that Hailsham showed his clownish side. On the party platform he rang a hand-bell and chanted: 'let us say to the Labour Party, seek not to inquire for whom the bell tolls – it tolls for thee.' And, as a sideshow, Hailsham made an annual ritual at party conferences of an early morning swim in the freezing sea – with photographers on hand. Spartan exercise is not just exhibitionism, though. It is part of his philosophy.

Macmillan seems to have come to regret assigning Hailsham to a meaningless sinecure. In 1963, forced by illness to retire as Prime Minister, for a few days he favoured the idea of Hailsham as his successor. In the public dog-fight that then broke out over the leadership, Hailsham, on the brink of tears, declared himself ready to surrender his peerage if nominated. But another peer, ready to make the same sacrifice, forestalled him: Lord Home. Two years later, when Heath replaced the disastrous Home, it seemed that the Thespian figure of Hailsham would disappear into limbo. Another generation had moved in.

On the grounds of academic record, Heath's decision to make Hailsham Lord Chancellor seemed just. The young Hogg made a brilliant start at Eton, and his performance at Oxford compared with that of Lord Birkenhead, the legendary advocate. He won a first in Mods and a first in Greats, became President of the Union and got a fellowship of All Souls' – just about the best equipment for either a legal or political career that Britain can give its elite.

But the academic records miss the full flavour of Hailsham's youth. He was not just the son of a great lawyer, but he was raised in a pressure-cooker of competitiveness with the sons of other great men. Randolph Churchill told the story of dinner parties where these sons would have to practise the art of public speaking under the critical gaze of their fathers. Birkenhead, Churchill, and the elder Hailsham had political *machismo*; their heirs were expected to live by the same values. Perhaps that kind of pressure sat permanently on Hailsham's back. Whatever the reason, his evident talents were shadowed by nagging doubts as his public life progressed. They were ultimately the cause of his failure to win the party leadership, and they were entirely to do with his temperament.

When his father died in 1950 Hailsham's automatic succession to the title made tangible a dread he had spoken of since adolescence, the impossibility of a peer becoming Prime Minister. He wrote to Clement Attlee, the Labour Prime Minister, demanding a reform (made years later) to allow an heir to revert to commoner by choice. This letter was so rude and peremptory that even the crusty senior Tory, Lord Salisbury, was moved to call it 'gratuitously insulting'.

At various times since then Hailsham has behaved a little wildly in public, sometimes on television. He was the first member of Macmillan's Cabinet to comment, on television, on the Profumo crisis, thus: 'A great party is not to be brought down because of a scandal by a woman of easy virtue and a proved liar.' This caused the Labour M.P. George Wigg to say in the House of Commons later: 'I would not pretend for one moment to be a Christian. If some of the ideas of Christianity which we have heard from Lord Hailsham are representative, then I confess that I am a pagan ...'

Macmillan, recalling private consultations over his own successor, has revealed his preference for either Iain Macleod or Hailsham – 'both men of great genius'. But the Cabinet demurred – 'I think many of our colleagues may have thought: well, they have genius, but in these very tricky, delicate, uncertain times we have to live in now, have they got enough judgment and balance?' For Hailsham it was the recurrent question.

Hailsham has a notoriously low boiling-point in argument. He is easily goaded into petulant, arrogant or emotional responses. Age has not mellowed him. He is a man driven by severe Calvinistic suspicions that moral and civil disorder are real threats to the state. His view of the Wilson years of the 1960s is doleful: he compares them to the state of the Weimar Republic and the French Third and Fourth Republics, and other countries 'which one way or another have gone down before the blast of dictatorship'. These views mark his public statements. As Lord Chancellor he did not withdraw into discretion. In a definitive speech to Young Conservatives at Margate in March 1973 he developed a new, even more alarming vision of the assembled threats to the security of True Brit:

> In what direction are world events pointing? The war in Bangladesh, Cyprus, the Middle East, Black September, Black Power, Angry Brigade, the Kennedy murders, Northern Ireland, bombs in Whitehall and the Old Bailey, the Welsh Language Society, the massacre in the Sudan, the mugging in the Tube, gas strikes, hospital strikes, go slows, sit-ins, the Icelandic cod war ...

Nobody else could quite so accurately have shown in one breath all the nightmares of the uneasy Custodian. No mention of Vietnam, but the Welsh Language Society ... the enemy of democracy was, he said, indiscipline: 'It is no use masking anarchy or indecisiveness under the bland names of liberalism or permissiveness.' It was not 'excessive authority' that was the greater threat, but 'the frustration of government by dissident minorities'. In other places and at other times it was Reds under the bed.

Hailsham did help to define the demonology of the Custodians, and gave an idea of why the lion had been so easily aroused by Richard Neville's flea. But how far was it really a collective paranoia, and how far his own private vision? No other member of the Heath Cabinet was so wild in his language. Hailsham was prepared to play on a simplistic notion of 'law and order' as a political lever, although in his case it was called 'liberty under the law'.

These issues easily pervert language. As the campus polemicist will carelessly use 'fascist', Hailsham uses 'dictator' to include forms of separatism like Welsh nationalism. The implication is that 'dictatorship' is a refusal to conform. In such a lexicon dissent easily becomes a crime, the crime of refusing to accept that minorities should trust the state to look after their interests in its infinite compassion and wisdom. But in Britain the state, and the judiciary, has grown insensitive to minorities, and does not offer equitable remedies for their grievances.

Many lawyers outside the judiciary were unsettled by Hailsham's intemperate language and political engagement. They were also troubled by some of his appointments to the judges' bench. Although by nature and ethic lawyers are a discreet profession, they began to speak out. Lord Goodman, a solicitor and ubiquitous power-broker, said of the *Oz* judgment (in a speech to Scottish lawyers in 1972): 'When a judge finds himself in the position of having to announce that he is not acquainted with the science of jurisprudence, and has never heard of the Professor of

Jurisprudence at Oxford, there must be something wrong.'

The courts reached their present condition under the supervision of Lord Hailsham. The Lord Chancellor makes the law-makers. He selects the judges. He is the one man in the country who sits at the confluence of the judiciary, the Executive, the Cabinet and the ruling party. He is a politician, a lawyer, an administrator and – one hopes – a man of impartial wisdom. An American President can, if helped by mortality, make the Supreme Court his own. So can a Lord Chancellor seed the benches with judges who reflect his own sympathies. Over a few years the climate of English law can be effectively conditioned by the Lord Chancellor's appointments.

In Hailsham's case the appointments are, he admits, a problem: 'I am reaching the stage when I am finding it less easy to discover professional judges and magistrates of sufficient experience and quality.' But one of his solutions seems irrational – a curtailment of the right to opt for a jury trial. Only 2 per cent of criminal cases go to a jury; the remainder are heard in magistrates' courts. Law administered by magistrates has become disturbingly capricious, with anomalies explicable only by regional and personal quirks. More and more defendants are choosing to elect for jury trial, a trend that exacerbates the creaking of the court machinery. The need to remedy this is the justification that Hailsham cites for limiting the access to jury trial. But his abolition of the right of the defence to know the occupation of jurors, carried out in the summer vacation with a minimum of consultation, suggests that, like Sir Robert Mark, he regards juries as too fallible.

Hailsham's mark on the law is that of a man with a driving sense of public duty, swept along by messianic prophecies and the slogans of Super-Brit. The preservation of British democracy now rested, he said in November 1973, on 'a return to patriotism, loyalty, public spirit and civic virtue', but conceded sadly that this creed was always answered by 'ridicule, unbelief, cynicism and sometimes outright hostility'. But Hailsham, at least, has never confused patriotism with racial purity.

Portrait of a Patriot : 2
Leading the nation back to its Valhalla

In his Homburg hat and three-piece suits, the Rt. Hon. J. Enoch Powell, M.P., is always armoured in the unbending formality of the English gentry. Not one layer is shed on even the hottest of days, nor is there ever a sign of sweat. It is the glacial composure that used to be mandatory among British public figures but no longer is; Powell retains it as though indicating his contempt for modern laxities. It was the same when he served in the Egyptian desert in World War II. While other officers – Montgomery, for example – created their own idiosyncratic battledress, Powell appeared with his belts waxed and brilliant, always the martinet and always the embodiment of the Indian Army officer.

But it is all a bit of a pose. He comes not from the rural shires where Kipling blonds were reared and bred, but from a middle-class family in the industrial 'Black Country' of the Midlands, a background stamped in his flat vowels. The clipped military moustache is grey now, and his skin parchment-white. Only the eyes, on the brink of being hypnotic, betray any sign of real energy. These are not the makings of a popular idol. And yet Powell is the one man who could make a new constituency of right and left, rich and poor. 'It is a subject', he says, 'which found me: I didn't go looking for it.' The subject is race, and he has made it his own.

Powell is more formidable as a hard-liner on race than anyone who has openly preached racism all his life. He is replete with the credentials of a mature political career; he cannot be written off as a freak. Even more, and this is something he relies on, he is always characterized as a man of superior intellect. A translator of Herodotus, scholarly, and acquainted with the richness of Greek civilization. How could such sophistication be aligned with a sentiment as crude as racism?

The belief in Powell's rigour of intellect survives some remarkable inconsistencies:

October 1964: 'I have and always will set my face like flint against making any difference between one citizen and another on grounds of his origin.'

November 1968: 'The West Indian or Indian does not, by being born in England, become an Englishman. In law he becomes a United Kingdom citizen by birth: in fact he is a West Indian or Asian still.'

None of the elements making up the chemistry of Enoch Powell seemed either unstable or fissionary until April 20th, 1968. The only fragile clue to some subterranean disturbance lay in his sense of Englishness. This surfaced briefly in a Parliamentary debate in 1953. The empire was dissolving into the 'Commonwealth', and the House of Commons was dealing with the Royal Titles Bill. The nomenclature of the monarchy had to be adjusted to its reduced status. Powell's beloved Indian Army had gone, and with it the mantle of Kipling and the heritage of the savages redeemed by the white man. The young Elizabeth was only months away from that flux of national sentiment, the Coronation. The spiritual levitation carried Powell away:

Sometimes elements which are essential to the life, growth and existence of Britain seem for a time to be cast into shadow, and even destroyed. Yet in the past they have remained alive; they have survived; they have come to the surface again, and they have been the means of a great flowering which no one has suspected. It is because I believe that, in a sense, for a brief moment, *I represent and speak for an indispensable element in the British constitution*, that I have spoken. (Italics mine)

Powell lamented the surrender of imperial power. Disembodied from the monarchy, his emotional rhetoric was hard enough to take. Directed as it was to the cause of the Hanoverian throne it was ethnically ridiculous and historically fallible. The Queen's blood is one-part German and her husband is a Greek immigrant. No matter. Powell's mind is gripped by a racial fantasy.

His perception of himself as the spokesman for an otherwise mute polity then sank out of sight for years, an ember waiting for a fresh breeze. On April 9th, 1968, the Labour government introduced the Race Relations Bill, a first feeble attempt to legislate against discrimination. Eleven days later, in a speech at Birmingham, Powell reacted. The legislation was, he said, aimed at the wrong people: 'They have got it exactly diametrically wrong. The discrimination and the deprivation, the sense of alarm and resentment, lies not with the immigrant population but with those among whom they have come and are still coming.'

Then, mixing the prospect of apocalypse with an emotive phrase of Blake's, he said: 'Time is running against us and them. With the lapse of a generation or so we shall at last have succeeded in reproducing in "England's green and pleasant land" the haunting tragedy of the United States.'

But perhaps the most incendiary part of his speech was an anecdote about an old woman, supposedly living in Powell's constituency in Wolverhampton, in a street colonized by blacks until she was surrounded by them. To terrorize her into moving out, said Powell, the blacks had smashed her windows, she had been called a racialist by 'charming, wide-eyed, grinning piccaninnies' and, as a final gesture, excrement had been stuffed through her letter-box.

Assiduous research after Powell's speech failed to substantiate either the story or the woman. Powell had carefully attributed them to 'a correspondent in Northumberland' – a county remote from Powell's constituency. Powell later conceded that he had not himself checked back with the 'correspondent' to authenticate the story.

Because of this speech, Edward Heath sacked Powell from the Tory Shadow Cabinet. But political exile turned into political licence. On his own, without further party constraints, he could serve as the catalyst for all the so-far unchannelled racial fears. More important, Powell had done something which no leader of an extremist sect could have achieved: because of his status he had made respectable, overnight, opinions which until that moment were only whispered in the shadows of ignorance and fear.

As Powell developed his theme, becoming more cautious with anecdotes but more apocalyptic in his predictions, all manner of other pestilences came out from under rocks. Some were new in name and virulence, others warmed-up versions of an old broth. Powell had made for himself a political constituency, but one that was sometimes unpalatable even to him. He took particular care to keep clear of overt fascists in quasi-military gear. Though a cynic might think otherwise, Powell's aversion to brown shirts was not feigned. He had not fought for Albion against Hitler, only a generation later to embrace fascism. To call him a fascist is too simplistic, the same carelessness with labels that afflicts a modern campus where the memories are unschooled. Powell didn't need the fascists; they needed him.

To the black Britons, perhaps even more than for their parents, the inequities of British life can be the source of something more violent than disenchantment. What are they to make, for example, of Powell's 'final solution', that they should be persuaded to 'go back' to countries which they have never known? The shadow of Enoch Powell hangs over these people as the harbinger of an increasingly insecure future. Powellism's worst side is the tacit consent by which it flourishes, extending to the highest places. The more anonymous his admirers, the more influential they tend to be. Three millionaires, described as 'major City and industrial leaders', embarked on a campaign to spread Powell's doctrine more effectively through the land. As always, Powell refused to be drawn into any overt alliance, content that these propagandists should do his work for him. Splendid isolation is his style.

Powell's speeches give fluency to the most primitive instincts of the inarticulate and barely literate. His first immigration speech in 1968 produced an avalanche of mail. There were 100,000 letters in support, only 800 against; nothing was more instrumental in making this *his* issue. Of a representative sample of 3,400 of the letters, analysed by independent scrutiny, only 71 could be classified as openly racist. By far the most common fear – expressed by 1,128 of the sample – showed the same kind of curious hyper-patriotism, the froth of True Brit, which Powell manifested in his speech on the Royal Titles Bill. They were worried that 'Englishness' was being undermined. 'No Briton', said one, 'wants to see his traditional way of living, the country he has loved and fought for, lose its identity, and particular character, through the over great acceptance of too many peoples of quite different cultures and ways of life.' More bluntly, another described the immigrants as 'a non-British population which cares nothing for our traditions.'

It may be unduly cautious not to brand these sentiments as racism. They certainly reflect a morbid patriotism, the gripe of the dispossessed. It afflicts Powell himself, and may even be the trigger of his bile. Those who know him in private moments say that, after a night in the House of Commons listening to the bleak managerial imperatives of his party leaders he will slump disconsolately into a cab, shaking his head and muttering 'our poor country'. Marooned away from the decision-making and surrounded by admiring boors whom he despises, Powell feels more and more like the only man who perceives his people's peril. It is the kind of isolation that can easily turn a man's head.

But Powell is not unhinged. He does not seek to create a master race of blue-eyed blonds. His England is for the mongrel English, as long as they are white. He seems un-aware that it is the worst instincts of the English that he articulates, not the best. His has become the most divisive voice in the land, far more fundamental and arousing than conflicts of ideology. His only apparent solution is not healing but excision. And his own intolerance is sustained by a misplaced tolerance on the part of others. He is isolated but not discredited, rebuked but not outlawed. Powell presents the ultimate and infinitely resistible dilemma of the democratic society: whether or not to tolerate the intolerable. In Britain the right of an urbane and erudite politician to put forward extremist arguments is still thought essential to free debate, and valued above the rights of a coloured minority to themselves share in the political processes. The benefit of the doubt has been generously extended to Powell. He has used up every inch of earlier respect and reputation. The only way of seeing him in the truest light is to be black.

Powell may well see himself as a kind of English de Gaulle, carried along as de Gaulle was by a surge of reactionary instincts which he secretly despises, but ready to use it to propel him into power. His *hauteur*, like de Gaulle's, rests on a higher sense of destiny. He does not plan to appear leading a column of racist shopkeepers, and certainly not a rabble. He is a man for All England, when it wakes up to reassert its independence and rediscover that spark in its genes. He is waiting for that, for then he will be called. He is the Last Patriot.

Powell feels that inside the Common Market Britain will disappear into a new European state 'as one province along with others'. In a speech at Stockport in June 1973 he offered this as the rubric of his ambition: 'Independence, the freedom of a self-governing nation, is in my estimation the highest political good, for which any disadvantage, if need be, and any sacrifice, are a cheap price. It is worth living for; it is worth fighting for; and it is worth dying for.' The truth may well be that Powell's adoption of the racial bandwagon is really a piece of opportunism, the first recruiting-drive of a man collecting his legions under a false banner, keeping a grander strategy to himself. What does it matter if these legions are allowed a few skirmishes on the way, if a few immigrants are softened up? The army is still incomplete, but the first steps have been taken on the road towards that vision of an England once more in the hands of the English.

Ultra Brit:
A long steady backslide to racism

The film is called 'England, Whose England?' It sounds as though it might be some flight of pastoral fancy by Alfred Lord Tennyson. But it is no whimsy. The faces of the people who pack meeting halls to see it are embittered. They are people who fear a nightmare that the film brings to life.

It is made in the manner of a documentary, slick and urgent. There are long-focus shots that foreshorten perspective so that a street of people seems like a compressed mass. In these street scenes many of the faces are black. The commentary runs:

> Immigrant families move in, whites move out. The Asians take trade away from white shops, and the white shops close down. Asian traders don't make any genuine contribution to the community as a whole. They remit forty million pounds a year to their home countries. (*Pause*). White women have trouble getting hospital beds ...

'England, Whose England?' is an insidious exercise in racial poison, but it tours the meeting-hall circuit untroubled. No law restrains this kind of propaganda.

Another scene is in Bradford, a city with a large Asian population. Bradford's business is wool, the making of many fine cloths. The county emblem is the White Rose. In this film a man says: 'It's a long time since the White Rose flowered in these streets.' (*Cut-away shot to Asians.*) A woman says: 'Our poor lads are fighting in Ireland while our own country is being invaded.' And winding to its apocalyptic climax, the commentary says: 'It is the fifty-ninth minute of the eleventh hour. (*Pause.*) To discriminate does not mean to hate, but to choose.'

Applause.

The twisted semantics of the final slogan are the hallmark of the Monday Club, the most extreme faction connected to the Tory party, and sponsors of the film. 'England, Whose England?' shows how much licence is given in Britain to inflammatory racism, so long as it comes from whites. In the shades from grey to black which are the spectrum of the ultra-right in Britain, the Monday Club is on the lighter fringe. Its importance is as a link in a chain. On one side the Monday Club connects with the Parliamentary Tories and even with Tory ministers; on the other, a more blurred edge, it leads directly to groups which were once dismissed as a lunatic fringe, but which now look more substantial.

A seam of fascism runs through modern British politics, part underground and part visible. It has always seemed unstable: waxing, waning, mutating. But it is always there, and cannot be underrated. Like any extreme, Ultra Brit may at times seem comic, but it is no joke. It is judged best by the issues on which it makes a stand.

Before World War I there was a strain of extreme and cranky nationalism that pursued the phantom of an international conspiracy of Jewish financiers. Englishness was threatened by their manipulations, or so the theory went. These propagandists included the Roman Catholic novelists and pamphleteers, G. K. Chesterton and Hilaire Belloc. Bernard Shaw called them Chesterbelloc, like a two-headed monster. Behind their hysteria was a struggle between the old money and the new, the English gentry and the Edwardian plutocracy. It was also a kind of simple-minded anti-Semitism.

Between the wars this strain of anti-Semitism fused with the formal fascism of those Britons, and there were many, who fell under the spell of Mussolini and Hitler. This movement peaked in Oswald Mosley's British Union of Fascists and the Anglo-German Friendship League, which spilt over into the eccentric salon of Nancy, Lady Astor. Pressure from these sources reached the British Cabinet even after war was declared against Hitler. A group of eight Tory peers blamed the war on Jewish-controlled newspapers, and wanted to appease the Germans. Churchill sent them away with a flea in their ear, but the sentiment did not disappear. It lay dormant, like an incubating virus. Its next appearance was years later, and the cause was the fall of empire.

This might have been transitory, a doomed rearguard action fought to the memory of Kipling and the music of Gilbert and Sullivan. But it was regenerated by the emergence of immigration as an issue. The catalyst of diehard colonialism was the League of Empire Loyalists, founded by A. K. Chesterton, a cousin of G.K. and formerly a founder of Mosley's Fascists. The League was little more than a hysterical gadfly buzzing about the rump of the Tory party. In 1962 Chesterton's organizer in the Midlands, Colin Jordan, quit to form the British National Socialist Movement. At first it seemed a lame-duck re-run of Mosley, with Nazi uniforms and the old Nordic dream: 'The only basis for Britain's future greatness is Aryan, predominantly Nordic blood. It is the first duty of the state to protect and improve this blood.'

The state's reaction was to slap Jordan in gaol for leading a para-military organization. His surviving lieutenants learned the lesson. They moved with less flamboyance and more purpose towards a new and clear-cut target, the immigrants. Like Powell after them, the Fascists told unauthenticated stories about old women being molested and terrorized by blacks. Like Powell they invoked Blake's 'green and pleasant land', and warned that 1984 would see a 'mongrel Britain'.

By 1966, four of the ultra groups, including the League of Empire Loyalists, merged into a new block called the National Front. Chesterton remained its ingenuous figurehead until 1971. Waking up finally to the monster he helped to create, he confessed: 'I had had more than enough, after four years, of stamping out nonsense such as plots to set fire to synagogues. Two per cent of the National Front are really evil men ...'

The Front developed political savvy. It acted as *agent provocateur* in volatile situations, especially racial conflicts. Anonymous thugs broke up political meetings with boot-stamping. And it was ready to catch the surge of feeling among the white *lumpen* proletariat that a black invasion was going to dispossess them of homes and jobs. National Front men went to Germany for reunions of ex-members of the S.S. The Germans endearingly called the Front's new leader, John Tyndall, the Führer. Tyndall aped Mosley in accent and style. But Mosley, skilfully rehabilitating his reputation as a political philosopher in Britain and the U.S.A., dismissed the Front as 'dwarfs masquerading in the uniform of dead giants' – unconscious of his implied nostalgia.

With a formal membership of around 10,000, the National Front is British Fascism without 'couth', a blunt and primitive instrument that catches the ugliest intemperance of the British character. It has been able to fan racism to the point where its candidates can collect up to 20 per cent of the vote in some local and national elections, in constituencies where immigrants are an issue. The Front thrives in that seedbed of racism, the Midlands. Sometimes its proletarian roots extend up into the lower middle class, where it makes tentative contact with the Monday Club. There is no natural sympathy between them; the class gulf is too strong. But it can be expedient to connect the chain.

The Front's support is visceral, as popular with Labour voters as Tory. The Monday Club is an orbiting remnant of galactic implosions as the Tory party underwent reformation. Part of this debris is vestigial colonialism, supporting the white man's last stand in Africa. Another part is a semi-coherent form of populism, resisting big business and big government. Yet another part is the familiar 'law and order' lobby, which includes a hard line against students and trade unions. All this would be definable as the classical hard core of conservatism by any name, ancient laments and fashionable fears interwoven. But there is a putrefying additive, racism.

Without this, the Monday Club could claim, within the generous British conventions, to be 'respectable'. With it, all the other causes of True Brit are tarnished.

When the Heath government took office six of its members belonged to the Monday Club and some, like Geoffrey Rippon, had great influence. Thirty Tory M.P.s were members. Few of them were closet Fascists, and as the racist fringe of the Monday Club gained a greater hold the ministerial membership dwindled, and many of the M.P.s resigned. None the less it is significant that powerful Tories stayed in the Club while it conducted some grotesque essays in racism like 'England, Whose England?' Apparently only the preservation of a political career, rather than revulsion at these tactics, caused them to drop the Monday Club.

The most significant fact about the British right is what is not there – a leader. The grey of the Monday Club, splitting itself into darker factions, and the black of the National Front are bridgeable, as were the Waffen S.S. and the old Junker leadership of the German General Staff. But there is, as yet, nobody able or willing to carry the torch. Powell, the apparent candidate, does not fit. Where he is an academic theoretician, the Monday Club is predominantly non-intellectual and *petit bourgeoise*.

None the less, the racist right can reflect with satisfaction that if you have a strong enough cause you don't need a leader to get results. Ever since race surfaced as an issue in Britain, official policy has adopted the technique of the steady moral backslide. Every pressure from the extreme right, even when it was still represented only by cranks who were easily resisted on other issues, has been conceded.

Successive governments have introduced progressively tighter controls on immigration, and yet made only the most pathetic token measures against discrimination. Bigots have been consistently appeased while the blacks have been deflected from any credible political influence. The witch-hunting of immigrants has been unrestrained. Both covert and open discrimination is unimpeded on a wide scale. And any refusal by the blacks to passively accept these terms causes, even amongst the liberals, hysterical appeals to resist 'militancy'. It is pretty obvious where the successful militancy is.

The shifting terms of British cant are encapsulated by this Jamaican: 'In 1944 I was in the British air force fighting for freedom and democracy. In 1947 I became a settler in Nottingham. In the 1958 race riots I became a coloured man. In the 1962 Commonwealth Immigration Act I became a coloured immigrant. And in 1968 I became an unwanted coloured man.' It is hard to see British liberalism as anything but counterfeit. There is nothing in their records to distinguish the racial policies of the Tory and Labour parties. For example, the Macmillan government of the early 'sixties was reckoned to be as left-wing as any Tory government dare be. Macmillan decolonized Africa at a rate that enraged his right wing. The socially reforming core of that government was led by the Home Secretary, the patrician R. A. Butler. And yet it was Butler who enacted the 1962 Immigration Act, limiting immigrants to 30,000 a year and toughening the discretionary powers of the immigration authorities. Butler was the first victim of the right-wing backlash. He admits that it was one of the most bitterly fought episodes of his career. The lobby that forced his hand had its rump in the lower middle-class Tories of the industrial Midlands. This is Powell's own major power-base, but at that time he was dormant on the issue.

The racial folk-prejudices are at their worst in this area. The populations are largely the descendants of nineteenth-century immigrations of Irish and Scots. It was a proletarian

Tory candidate in the Midlands, Peter Griffiths, whose supporters in 1964 rallied to the slogan 'If you want a nigger for a neighbour, vote Labour.' In 1965, when Harold Wilson first reversed Labour's race policy and continued the path of backsliding, it was pressure from this same area that provoked him. Labour not only tightened controls, having earlier promised to repeal them, but also endorsed the idea of 'voluntary repatriation'.

More legislation in 1968, 1971 and 1973 has all but closed the door to immigrants. There is now a bi-partisan consensus upholding the line which began as the objective of a handful of right-wing extremists. In Nottingham, where the first (exaggerated) race riots took place in 1958, attitudes have been unchanged in fifteen years. A council-housing official unconsciously catches the spirit of British policy: 'People are prejudiced, and we must take their prejudice into account.' He is trying to justify the situation where whites are given priority over blacks in slum clearance.

There are now about one and a half million coloured people living in Britain – West Indians, Indians, Pakistanis, and Africans. Half a million of them are not immigrants. They were born British. And so it is galling for these British to see, as they often do, banners and posters saying 'Send Them Home'. They are at home. Or for them to hear a politician of liberal pretensions talking of 'repatriating' coloured families. Or to see civil servants expediently inventing new categories of people like 'Patrials', who are now the semi-British, no longer sharing the rights of the 'pure' native stock.

Looked at through the eyes and experience of blacks, immigrants or British-born, Britain is a place with an elaborately organized pattern of subtle and blatant discrimination. For the young it is embittering:

We've got nowhere to live – they shove the coloured people in dirty stinking flats they moved whites out of long ago. We can't get work. I've got a cockney accent, so over the phone they say OK. But when you go for an interview, they say fill in this form and that's the last you hear of it. We get framed. One day I was walking along and a car pulled up and four detectives jumped out, they grabbed me, searched me. They found two medical tablets I had to take. Then they took me down to the station and said 'You're not leaving here till we find a charge.' They re-searched me and 'found' some more tablets I'd never seen before. All we can do now is resort to violence. You're still going to get done if you do nothing, so you might as well inflict some real damage.

The unemployment rate amongst black youths, like this one in a London inner suburb, is three times the national average. Black Britons leave school after being given the expectations of a white society, only to find that immediately the equality they felt and enjoyed at school no longer applies. The immigrants were lured to Britain for one purpose: to become a new proletariat, to do work that has become too menial, too arduous or too dirty for white hands. From being subject races in the British colonies they are now subject races in the British domestic economy. They are indispensable and yet resented, an expedient resource and an ethnic irritation.

In a country with a long history of rinsing its conscience with words, the language of True Brit is versatile in euphemisms. Even trained social workers unthinkingly use the term 'host community' to describe the white population. The implication is that the blacks are there on sufferance, and as long as they abide by the conventions, rules and desires of their 'hosts' they can remain. If only they could, overnight, become white there would be no problem. Here, for an example, is a typical piece of double-think from the mouth of a Labour politician, Roy Hattersley, regarded as liberal, in the House of Commons in March 1965: 'We are all in favour of some sort of limitation on immigration. We all wholeheartedly oppose any sort of discrimination. We all wholeheartedly agree that there should be assimilation or adjustment, whichever word one prefers to use ... '

All the 'adjustments' have to be made by the blacks. And the dream of 'assimilation' persists, as though the ethnic characteristics are offensive, and must be surrendered as part of the price to be paid for enjoying life in this, the best of all possible worlds. It is not the careless white phrases which are really so appalling in themselves as much as the way they support the illusion of tolerance and liberalism. The assumed magnanimity of the British used to masquerade under the image of 'the Mother Country', that lady of empire whose children, of whatever colour, were so welcome. It now seems that the Mother Country was the Fatherland in drag: there is a hardness in her eye and her heart that betrays a change of gender.

One of Powell's constant themes, from the 1968 speech onwards, has been to suggest that British racial problems will follow the American pattern. It seems a specious analogy on the figures: Britain's coloured population is barely 3 per cent, compared to 12 per cent in the U.S.A. And since the British blacks are relative newcomers, they are not a group with a long history of suppressed civil rights. But these assumptions are deceptive.

The migrations of American blacks from the plantations of the south to the cities of the north is a paradigm of the migration of blacks from British colonial estates to the British industrial cities. The relative absence in Britain of a history of racial discrimination is more than compensated for by the endemic class discrimination, which mutates readily into ethnic discrimination. As with the American blacks when they arrived in the northern cities, the immigrants in Britain have been dumped where there are the worst housing and social conditions, cheek by jowl with an abused white proletariat, and depending on social services which cannot cope with the demands made on them.

The attitude of white authority to British blacks also has

striking echoes of what happened in the U.S.A. several generations ago. London's black population is now at about the same level as New York's during the great migration of 1910–20. In New York, Tammany Hall sought to handle the problem by creating the United Colored Democracy. The control lay with the white elites. Any blacks who failed to be placated by this arrangement were kicked out, stigmatized as 'militants'. The reaction of the British authorities has been identical. The most well-meaning effort has come from the voluntary initiatives of a traditional source of British social philanthropy, the liberal paternalists. As they once did in trying to cope with the abject miseries of the working class, the liberals have tried to neutralize the tension rather than offer real equality. During two decades of immigration the blacks have been encouraged to exist in their own cocoon and discouraged from direct political intervention.

The result is that there are no national black political leaders in Westminster (or anywhere else); no black officials at senior levels in trade unions (nor virtually at any level); no black managerial voices in industry; no blacks at any decisive level in the media (nor virtually at any level); very few practising black lawyers; and a derisory number of blacks in the police. Wherever it counts, the blacks are unrepresented. They are as good as disenfranchised.

While the white liberals talk of 'assimilation' and 'adjustment', the blacks are being isolated into powerless groups outside all the conventional white decision-holding bodies. In Britain the Liberal Hour has run out of time, and it has achieved nothing. Its impotence is in grim contrast to the countervailing forces.

Race-relations policy closely follows the pattern of British attitudes towards Northern Ireland. In both cases the normal civil rights of a substantial minority were withdrawn. In both cases the True Brit talent for temporizing creates the illusion of remedy. The instinct for repression is more influential than the instinct for the supposed saintly national virtues. The extremist minority is appeased, not those who are discriminated against. As with Northern Ireland, the pressure of smouldering resentment which this builds up is ineluctable. Britain has no special immunity to a racial disaster, however much the national conscience is paraded.

In 1685, 50,000 Huguenot refugees, driven from France by the persecutions of Louis XIV, settled in England. At first there was alarm that the immigrants were from an alien culture, and would be an economic threat. But, as a chronicler later conceded, 'instead of doing us a hurt it was soon discovered that they had proved a great and manifest blessing.'

16 *The Good Copper falls from grace*

The benign reputation of the British policeman has always rested to some extent on the belief that he is a bit dim-witted. The authors who helped to establish this legend took the middle-class view that a gifted amateur like Sherlock Holmes, Miss Marple, Lord Peter Wimsey, or even a priest like Father Brown, was a better detective than the pros. There is a strong streak of snobbery in this: in their manners and their accents the police have been presented as deferential proles. The Good Copper became a universal figure of both fun and respect. As late as 1971 the *New Yorker* magazine, a sort of emotional depository for Anglophilia, was able with conviction to run a profile of a London police constable as that same bicycle-riding, avuncular samaritan of fiction. To the inhabitants of Manhattan it was, of course, a calculated piece of escapism. Living with a siege mentality in the midst of soaring crime rates and dependent on an openly corrupt police force, the confirmation that the Good Copper apparently still existed must significantly have increased the already steady migration of New Yorkers to London.

The most generous thing to be said about that *New Yorker* profile is that its timing was bad. At just about the time that it appeared, London's allegedly impeccable police force was going through an unprecedented series of scandals. Moreover, it wasn't simply that corruption had become fashionable. The rot came out into the open only because it was forced there by the purging zeal of Sir Robert Mark. At the same time a market-research study reported in *The Times* of July 27th, 1973, revealed that half the adult population and two-thirds of the younger people are sufficiently disenchanted with the police to feel more fearful of them than respectful. Although the study's results were suppressed (ironically it was commissioned to aid police-recruiting) the shift in attitudes was obvious and irretrievable.

The seriousness of the fall of the Good Copper is still relative. Other countries assume that their police are corrupt, trigger-happy, brutal towards dissent, and immune to reform. All these traits are now at least visible in the British police, but so far they indicate a problem rather than an epidemic. It is only because the legend of incorruptibility was so strong that its collapse comes as a shock.

At the heart of that legend is Scotland Yard, controlling the 20,000 men of the Metropolitan Police. Things have gone badly wrong at the Yard. Two of its elite units, the Flying Squad and the Drugs Squad, were involved in corruption charges. The *known* rate of corruption in the London police is 1 per cent – incredibly low by New York standards but a disaster measured against the British tradition. In 1972 the number of policemen in London who admitted offences doubled, to 144. Eighty were, to use the official euphemism, allowed to 'retire early'.

The Yard was too ready to believe its own propaganda. The special squads developed into jealously preserved substates of their own. Organization and methods fell behind the more sophisticated developments in crime. Interdepartmental fights raged. The most intransigent group, the huge C.I.D., was corrupted but self-policing, so that men who fell under suspicion could be shunted out of sight to another division rather than be indicted. The honest police were demoralized by this kind of licence, and the arrogance and unscrupulousness of some of the leadership.

Sir Robert Mark was determined to clean up the Yard. For two years the old units fought to keep their identity and autonomy, a kind of star system dependent more on legends than results. But Mark dismantled the monolithic

C.I.D., and as a first step in matching the system to the crimes he set up a bank-robbery unit, which had early and spectacular successes. The Flying Squad, proudest of all the old units, survived only in name. It became a 200-man 'strategic force'. Because certain categories of crime, like truck hi-jacking, were among the most apparent British contributions to the Common Market, another unit was formed to co-ordinate with European police. There was a new intelligence system based on the constant surveillance of 'target' criminals.

All these reforms have improved efficiency, although at the expense of a great deal of disenchantment among the old guard. What they can't do is to make the police any more loved. And in the precarious relationship between the Good Copper and the British public, nothing is more sensitive than whether or not he should carry a gun. Rather than face this dilemma squarely, the police have now drifted to a point where their options are few – tacitly the London police is already an armed force.

It is an agonizing issue. British criminals once abhorred firearms as the sign of an unprofessional and unstable temperament. This is still true of the small fry. But the new, highly organized and mobile gangs with targets like banks and bullion shipments face determined resistance in which only guns are, in their view, decisive. And since the young hit-men have taken to using amphetamines to boost their nerves, things are increasingly hair-raising. An unarmed copper is desperately vulnerable.

The British police have practised 140 years of self-denial in the argument of whether or not to meet arms with arms. The idea of cops and criminals shooting it out in city streets is alien to the British experience. In Australia, which takes many of its habits and traditions from Britain, the police resorted to guns, with the result that they face a much more violent crime war than the British do. In Britain the compromise has been, without any open assent or debate, to limit the arms either to an anticipated need, or to special units trained in their use. In 1970 the police were issued with guns on 1,072 occasions; by 1972 the figure had more than doubled. And at the end of that year, by the kind of coincidence that was inevitable sooner or later, there was the first public shoot-out.

A copper on his way to guard a London embassy walked right into a bank raid. One of the gang fired at him with a shotgun; simultaneously the copper fired back, fatally wounding the raider. This incident revealed the existence of Scotland Yard's Special Patrol Group, which patrols in unmarked vehicles. It includes forty men who regularly carry guns. In this episode the public's sympathy was with the police. But a month later the same unit was involved in a less impressive action.

Two armed Special Patrol Group men faced three young Pakistanis staging a political protest at the Indian High Commission. The Pakistanis were brandishing guns, and refused to surrender. The S.P.G. men fired eleven shots, all but one of the rounds in their guns. Two of the Pakistanis were killed. Their 'guns' were toys sold in Woolworths at 65p. each. The Pakistanis probably believed the legend that British cops would not shoot to kill. It was the judgment of a matter of seconds, not easy on either side, but the bluff was fatal. S.P.G. men carrying .38 Smith and Wesson revolvers, each with six rounds in the magazine and another six at the ready, are a new phenomenon. A line has been crossed; there is no going back.

Asian community leaders wondered whether the police would have been quite so trigger-happy if the raiders had been white. It is an understandable question. After the agonizing over firearms, the most critical issue in the social role of the British police is their attitude to blacks. The record is bleak. Researchers have found that in the mind of the Good Copper coloured people are 'permanently in the area of suspicion'. In one sense, the police's role in race relations is thankless. Whether they deserve it or not, they are regarded by the blacks (particularly those born in

Britain) as the most immediate agent of a society that has cheated them. The Good Copper is the lightning-conductor for grievances for which he is not to blame.

In the absence of any other adequate and trained community service, the police are expected to be social workers of great sensitivity when they face racial problems. And yet their preparation for this role, even supposing they accept it, has been minimal. The police policy is muddled and ambivalent. In one West Indian neighbourhood in London, Brixton, the police had some success with an exercise to explain themselves to the blacks. But only weeks later, with no apparent provocation, the Special Patrol Group descended on the same area and began frisking blacks in the street, completely negating the public-relations effort.

In Liverpool, a city with a history of successive migrations of Irish, Scots, Chinese, West Indians, and Asians, a courageous policewoman went on B.B.C. radio to expose this story:

> In certain police stations, particularly in the city centre, brutality and drug planting and harassing of minority groups takes place regularly. I witnessed a police sergeant attack a teenage youth who had reported to the station on parole. The sergeant poured insults on the youth, picked him up by the coat lapels and banged his head against the wall several times, before throwing him into a chair. The youth was then dragged out to a police jeep and driven away. After hearing the word 'agriculture' used on a number of occasions I asked what it meant. The reply was – 'planting, but you can leave that to us.'

This might be music to the ears of the National Front, whose literature attributes all violent crime to blacks, but every piece of evidence of this kind – and there are many – discredits the police both as the glue in society and as the agents of the law. In truth, the crime rate amongst blacks is no higher than amongst whites, and in many immigrant communities – particularly Asian – it is substantially lower.

The Chief Constable of Leeds, for example, says: 'Immigrant areas are less of a problem to us than the skinheads or the crombies' (two brands of white teenage thug). These salient statistics are buried under white prejudice; both the courts and the media build up frightening images of black muggers without bothering to check the facts.

An obvious palliative would be the recruitment of black policemen. But this has been studiously neglected. The first black copper did not appear until 1965. By 1972 there were still fewer than 40 – 0·043 per cent of the total police force. One West Indian copper in London says: 'When you join the force you keep your friends and lose your acquaintances.' The suspicion is so heavy that a black in uniform feels like an Uncle Tom. As one black community leader puts it: 'I could not see myself becoming part of an institution that in every respect seems to be bent on keeping us down and molesting us.'

As the trust of the public in the police ebbs away, the police cover their tracks effectively. For most complaints against police conduct they act as their own judge and jury. Only allegations of criminal misconduct are referred outside, and then to the Director of Public Prosecutions, who is closely connected to the police, rather than an independent scrutineer. In 1971 there were 4,314 complaints against the London police alone. Only 145 were acted upon. Blacks have found it impossible to be heard. Out of 37 cases which were sifted from 155 complaints made to the Jamaican High Commission, not one was said to have any substance.

Attempts to put the complaints procedure into independent hands have met a stone wall. A review carried out by the police themselves was never published. Another attempt in 1973 was deflected when the government offered a 'study'. The idea this time is a version of that Scandinavian fashion, the Ombudsman, already cynically devalued in Britain. This version would even lack the power to call for papers and witnesses. He would be a 'last resort', to review the reviewers, who would be ... you guessed it, the police.

Complaints against the London police are rising by nearly 30 per cent a year.

In 1829, when Colonel Charles Rowan and Richard Mayne created the first police force, their priority was the simple Victorian one of protecting life and property and, as they put it in their first manifesto, 'the preservation of public tranquillity'. The copper is falling from grace now as both the social pressures intensify and criminals become much smarter.

All the skills of modern white-collar crime are attracted to London. The City of London is the biggest financial centre outside Wall Street, with weak defences against smart operators. Beyond the traditional delinquencies of the League of Gentlemen, the white-collar crime rate is soaring. The known rate of company fraud is about £50m. a year, but the real figure is probably much higher. This is the province of Scotland Yard's Fraud Squad, under-manned, ill-equipped, overworked, and hampered by territorial disputes.

The Fraud Squad is probably the branch of the Yard which has been most outpaced by the smart new crimes. Its men seem like janitors trying to eavesdrop on the life-style of the executive suite. They are recruited from the general ranks of the police force, without a background in the world and techniques of business, and remote from the ethos of international corporate crime. The main part of the Squad operates out of Scotland Yard, but there is a separate section in the City itself. Disputes between the two are compounded by rivalries between the police and the Department of Trade and Industry's own inspectors. The ministry drafted Peter Walker's cosmetic new company law, and will insist on policing in its own way, though it has a record of inertia.

Fraud is an abstruse crime, lacking the social impact of violence, and yet it is the major growth-area in British criminology. The casual lawlessness of the City of London is amateur in comparison. Big-roll gambling, fine-art faking and robberies, and now elaborate company swindles make London a mecca for crime syndicates. Crime is still not flagrant on the streets, but behind closed doors True Brit is being taken for the mug it is.

A police force that is losing behaves in the same way as a country that is losing. It turns nasty and it turns in on itself. It is true that the Good Copper still plays veterinary surgeon, midwife, health visitor, mental welfare officer, surrogate parent, deterrent to suicides, tourist adviser, and buffer between bureaucrat and citizen – and that he performs many private acts of heroism beyond his formal responsibilities. He is in the front line when the bombs go off. But it would be sad to have to admit that the measures by which his legend was once remarkably credible are now too stringent.

If the British were selling True Brit only to themselves it would be bad enough, but they are out there selling it to other people. They have to: it's export or perish. The point of creating the corporate state was to gear up lagging industry to compete in the international markets. But a lot of that effort has come to nought. True Brit has over-reached himself.

Surrender of the empire was a *fait accompli*. But the state of mind behind it did not disappear; it lives on as a commercial and technical fantasy. The really big disasters in the selling of True Brit – and they are epic – are all traceable to this delusion. The country cannot match its efforts to its resources because, in doing so, it would have to admit the unthinkable: it is no longer the champ.

In 1945 Britain, despite being drained by war, was ahead of America in computers, jet engines and radar, and saw much sooner the potential of nuclear energy for power stations. In all of these she has now been decisively outdistanced by America and other countries. One of the few remaining ideas to support the notion of British inventive primacy, the linear-induction motor, has been sabotaged by government ineptitude. Technology in Britain has been made risible by the heroic demands made of it in the name of True Brit, and by consistently unprofessional management.

It was the old Desert Fox himself, Field-Marshal Erwin Rommel, who noticed his adversary's failing. It was, he said, part of the British character to produce good ideas and then fail to execute them. Rommel was smart enough to steal the theory of tank warfare from the British and use it devastatingly against them. The British might have taken the tip, and specialized in selling ideas to people more able to do justice to them. Instead, in the frenzy of True Brit, they have tried to be both innovator and seller, with lamentable results. It does, as Rommel suspected, seem to be a flaw of character.

The Impossible Dream 1 : Rolls Royce goes berserk

Three seemingly enduring symbols of True Brit were once the Bank of England, the rock of Gibraltar, and Rolls Royce. In any all-purpose kit of patriotic totems, these had no equal. The Bank stood for the sanctity of the pound sterling, the rock for imperial impregnability, and Rolls Royce for things that worked and went on working. All three have fallen. But the collapse of Rolls Royce was the hardest to take.

When David Ogilvy renewed the Rolls legend in America in the 1950s with the slogan 'at 60 m.p.h. the only sound you'll hear is the ticking of the clock' he had what every ad-man dreams of: a product seemingly so good that it hardly needed selling. The Rolls had something more than superlative craftsmanship and engineering excellence. It had mystique.

But the car division was an increasingly minor part of the Rolls business. The company's fortunes depended on aero-engines. Rolls were the first to make the jet engine a reliable proposition. For two decades their jets were unsurpassed. But there came a point, for Rolls and for Britain, where going one jump further in technology came perilously close to getting out of their depth – financially and technically. It was the crunch of matching ambition to resources. Going beyond that point involved Rolls in doing something wholly against their character. They had to be reckless.

Rolls alone can't be blamed for this. They were pulled along in the collective hallucination. The pride of True Brit was at stake.

The cause of Rolls's downfall was their deal with Lockheed to produce the RB211 engine for the Tristar. To the British it meant breaking into the American domestic market and cocking a snook at their toughest opposition. When the deal was signed the reaction was like a national virility-rite. Even normally sane newspapers went into a chauvinistic delirium. 'BRITAIN IS BETTER THAN ANY-ONE ELSE IN THE WORLD', said *The Observer*. And the Duke of Edinburgh, a tireless optimist, wired the firm: 'Delighted you have pulled off the deal.'

Two years later the British Prime Minister called President Nixon in Washington on the hot line. There is no public record of the conversation. But perhaps it may have gone something like this:

EDWARD HEATH. Er, I say Mr President, I have some rather bad news. Rolls Royce is going bankrupt.

RICHARD NIXON. Who?

HEATH. Rolls Royce ... you know, *the* Rolls Royce.

NIXON. Too bad. What should I do about it, Prime Minister?

HEATH. Well, Mr President, it looks as if Lockheed are going to have a new plane without any engines.

NIXON. Is that right? Could you make that perfectly clear?

HEATH. We've put about two hundred million dollars into Rolls and the engine still won't come right. I can't see how we alone can do anything more. But perhaps if Lockheed means anything to you ...

NIXON. You're damn right it does. It's a Californian company.

HEATH. I thought you might get the point.

NIXON. See here, Prime Minister, I can't guarantee you anything, but I'll have you transferred to the Department of Defence.

HEATH. The Department of *Defence*?

NIXON. I have a man in there called Packard. He'll help you all he can. He has access to funds. With an election coming up we can't have an airplane in California without any engines. But I wish you guys would wise up and get out of the aerospace business ...

Packard and Heath talked, and in the austere language of the official record, 'No undertakings were given on either side and the two governments agreed to keep in touch.' It was a frosty moment in Anglo-American diplomacy. The British felt they had been mousetrapped by the Lockheed deal; the Americans felt that Rolls Royce had been spectacularly inept in its calculations. But Lockheed had to be kept in the air for much the same reasons that Rolls Royce had to be saved: the political blowback of failure was a more acute pressure than sheer cost.

Although the official British inquiry tried to palm off the blame on the Rolls executives, the real guilt was as much in Whitehall as in the Rolls works at Derby. The civil servants overseeing the production of the RB211 included, as it happened, Sir Robert Marshall, who had been so generous in dispensing the North Sea oil licences. There were two peculiarities about the contract between Rolls and Lockheed: nobody in Whitehall had even seen it until months after it was signed, and British-government aid had never before been advanced for a project covered by a contract signed in the American courts.

The aberration of Rolls's throwing caution to the winds was rather like a village parson getting drunk and riding his bicycle recklessly. So much did they covet the Lockheed deal that they fixed a price for each engine without allowing for either inflation or technical problems – and they accepted punitive penalty clauses if they failed to meet performance goals and delivery dates. Yet when the contract was signed the RB211 was little more than a gleam in its designers' eyes, an engine which in order to work had to prove a number of unproven concepts. Immaculate conception is not a common feature of the aerospace business, not even at Rolls Royce.

In reality, Rolls had gone berserk. They were glued to a contract they couldn't meet. They had been wildly overoptimistic on the development programme. They had even glossed their accounts, writing down an inventory as assets to conceal a serious cash shortage. Lockheed, with troubles of its own, could be merciless with such a contract, and was.

Under this pressure something happened that must have made Sir Henry Royce, the engineering genius, spin in his grave. Rolls cut corners. A first batch of RB211 engines had been faulty, but promising. A second batch, rushed through to try to meet the Lockheed deadline, was disastrous. The fine engineering tolerances necessary had not been met. Performance was so bad, with hot gases leaking, that the engines had to be rebuilt. It was mortifying for the self-respect of the Rolls engineers, and mortal for the company.

A powerful *zeitgeist* inhabited Rolls, the spirit of genius at the workshop bench. For years the engineers feared that the company's original spark could easily be snuffed out if corporate organization superseded the worth of individuals. Even when a £12m. I.B.M. computer-bank was installed, the tradition of the maverick engineer was allowed to persist. The RB211 dénouement was more than the unravelling of a mystique – it was the end of the road for 'seat of the pants' judgment in a business that had thrived on it.

The RB211 had sucked in money and burned it in much the same way that it was supposed to suck in air with the same impunity. Its final cost was £200m., most of it public money. Sir Robert Marshall, bruised but still a model of civil service sang-froid, admitted that at the time he was funding the project he regarded Rolls to be as safe as the Bank of England. It was an unhappy comparison, as well as a revealing remark. Rescuing Rolls buried Edward Heath's declared commitment to non-wetness. There were plaintive statements like 'our reputation as a trading nation and as leaders in technology' and of Rolls Royce's 'high technical reputation'. A more believable epitaph was spoken by Sir Robert Marshall: 'It would be quite silly for anybody with knowledge of these things to suppose that mishaps on a considerable scale could not occur again.' He should know.

He was also involved in another flight of True Brit which makes Rolls Royce look like a minor plumbing error.

The Impossible Dream 2 : Up, up and away in the Great White Bird

It has it all: rampant True Brit, anti-Americanism, Anglo-French chauvinism, technical overreach, Executive conceal-ment, the massive diversion of public funds into the accounts of wayward corporations, contempt for the environment, the pursuit of narrow political self-interest, and the gross distortion of social priorities. The Concorde, the Anglo-French supersonic airliner, eclipses any other misadventure in the pursuit of national glory. In more rational times it would be seen as the definitive scandal of its kind, the chilling proof that technology can subvert sanity and the democratic processes.

The Concorde covers a decade and a half of European history. This life-span is the key to its survival. It shows how such a project can outlive its creators – governments, departments and dreamers. When some of its begetters realized their error, the Thing had taken on a life of its own. It could not be stopped.

Its origins are political. The Concorde grew directly from the mentality which plotted the 1956 invasion of Suez, the most conspicuous post-war example of Anglo-French collusion. Only six years separated Suez and the signing of the pact to build the plane, and the planning had started much earlier. A strong motive linking Concorde with Suez, easily underrated, is the resentment in London and Paris at American colonialism, military and commercial. In 1956 the Sixth Fleet sailed across the Anglo-French invasion fleet as an intimidating warning, although it was actually Eisenhower's threat to bankrupt the British Treasury that ended the adventure. The last spasm of empire was over.

Since then Boeing wrapped up the world market for jets, pioneered by the British Comet and the French Caravelle. And so, at the end of the 1950s, the French and the British decided to do something which even the Americans were wary of: to leap-frog a generation ahead, from subsonic to supersonic flight. Some of the most expert voices were sceptical. Lord Brabazon, the first man in Britain to qualify as a pilot, predicted that the Concorde's costs would be ruinous, that it would be inhumanly noisy, and that, even if it worked, all that would be achieved was that 'a few businessmen might arrive two hours sooner in New York'. He also pointed out, with feeling, the dismal record of the British aviation industry: 'An aircraft named after me was three years late. The engines did not arrive until three years after the project was scrapped.' A prophet is not without honour ...

At £200m., split between the two countries, the first prediction of Concorde's costs seemed to be the price of getting Britain into the Common Market: de Gaulle would be reassured that the British had finally turned their backs on perfidious Columbia. Even that didn't work: the British only got into Europe over the General's dead body.

The signatories of the Concorde agreement were exceptionally light-headed, even for conspirators. Costs were not discussed by the Treasury or the French Ministry of Finance. More fatally, there was no break-clause allowing either country to eject themselves in a high-speed stall. So that when Harold Wilson prepared to kill the Concorde in its tracks, he discovered that it would probably cost £200m. in the international court. By then there were all the signs of an incipient disaster: escalating costs, technical overconfidence, sloppy management. Eight years later, Roy Jenkins, who had been Wilson's Aviation Minister in 1966, noted ruefully: 'Perhaps we should have been more stubborn even when confronted by that cliff face.'

From the signing of the contract to its first flight the Concorde ran through four governments, two Tory and two Labour; five ministers; and, consecutively, five ministries. Its only consistency, and the reason for its resilience, lay in the management of the Custodians. Under cover of the bureaucratic mergers in Whitehall, political indetermination, and corporate voracity, the project could run fast and loose, and did. By 1969 it had swallowed £730m.; by 1972 £900m.; by 1973 well over £1,000m. Parliament supinely voted the funds without being given any of the information essential for judging how it was being spent. The plane had a paralysing power over the political will.

Certainly, technology never created a more impressive seductress. The Concorde's line is liquid and faultless to the eye, a dart to pierce the heart of sober doubt. From its needle-nose to the tips of its tulip-curved wings it seems to have consummated the aesthetics of the mind and the computer. With the nose canted down to improve the pilots' vision the Concorde has an almost anthropomorphic quality. But it has a split personality: beguiling in repose and barbaric in action. Once the four engines ignite, the earth shakes, the ears burst, the air around the plane distorts into searing bubbles of heat, and black, smearing smoke flowers into cloud and then dissipates into a cloying, sooty film. Even when it is invisible, a sliver of boiling metal at 50,000 feet, the Concorde leaves its mark on the ground in a wake of sonic boom which smashes windows and cracks walls.

The first serious crack in the display of profligate nationalism which kept the plane alive came in New York. Despite a sustained assault by French and British salesmen and politicians, Pan Am and T.W.A. didn't buy. The salesmen were so desperate to get planes in American livery that they offered to 'loan' Concordes to the airlines. That didn't work.

True Brit can turn very ugly when it is cornered. The success of Concorde demanded, it seemed, unquestioning patriotism. British air-correspondents were mostly brainwashed into flag-waving support. In January 1973, when Andrew Wilson of *The Observer*, one of the few sceptics among them, predicted cancellation of the American 'options' on Concorde Michael Heseltine, the British Aerospace Minister, furious with affronted patriotism, told M.P.s that the story was 'a fabrication'. Within days it was confirmed. Parliament went along with the fraud. It meekly swallowed ministerial refusals to reveal what was really going on: 'It would not be in the interests of the project to reveal the figures. That has been the view of every Minister.'

Not in *whose* interests? *The project's?*

Behind the cover-up were some strange blunders. For example, the pilots' seats. Not, on the face of it, items of challenging technology. Originally costed at £54,000, the seats finally came out at £409,000. The Concorde crewmen will be nothing if not cushioned.

With Pan Am and T.W.A. out of the game, the national-flag airlines of B.O.A.C. and Air France had to have Concorde rammed down their throats. B.O.A.C. said that operating it would bankrupt them. They were 'loaned' £135m. by the government, an offer they couldn't refuse. Even without taking that into account, the real cost of each plane delivered to B.O.A.C. and Air France, including development costs, was £215m., a sum fit to stagger even the most hardened free-spender of the military–industrial bonanza. In that way at least, the British and the French were shaping up to the Americans.

The only really tangible benefit from the Concorde was its impact on the cash flow of its two builders, the British Aircraft Corporation and Aerospatiale. The fact that B.A.C. makes any profit at all is due largely to the involuntary charity of the British taxpayer. Both Concorde and B.A.C. are kept afloat by military contracts.

The mutability of money, notorious in all enterprises of this kind, has been greatly extended by Concorde. Just as in the cosmic measures of light years, the familiar and mortal dimension of money cannot be translated to provide a sense of values to aerospace artifacts. The awe that strikes a man standing before an Apollo rocket is a mixture of humility and incomprehension. If told that it requires X billion dollars to encase three men in aluminium, or even half a billion dollars to provide them with as recognizable an object as a television camera, we have to suspend all our normal faculties of reasoning. This anaesthetizing effect cannot be underestimated in any record like that of Concorde. Because money loses its normal dimension the senses are lulled so that the enormity of the experience is easily diminished.

The Concorde's target date for airline service slipped back steadily to 'early 1976'. Two years before it was due to fly its first passengers it had cost the British taxpayers at least £750m. out of a known total of £1,300m. Successive governments have misled Parliament on costs; each time they have had to find more money, and each time they have got it. The French have not been so reticent. On the day a British minister withheld the price being asked of airlines for the plane it was being released to the Press in Paris; on another occasion the Tory government refused to disclose development costs, only for them to be revealed to the French Chamber of Deputies.

The French are far less furtive in their chauvinism than the British; the British felt pangs of remorse after Suez, the French felt merely betrayed by the Anglo-Saxons. In everything from atomic tests to cheese the French national personality has hubris, however preposterous the cause. They have no need to conceal their motives because public opinion is with them. True Brit, on the other hand, is always haunted by acts of disloyalty, always feels the sceptics snapping at its heels. The nation is not at one on its most flagrant adventures. Its rulers become mean and draconian when responding to complaint. To complain is to be wet, to be wet is to do down the product, and to do down the product is industrial and commercial sabotage, or even treason.

The heavily censored and intermittent public reports on Concorde are peppered with weary admonitions and empty vows of reform like 'revised procedures', 'radical reorganization', and 'investigation to remedy the defect'. One of these reports noted: 'It would not be practicable or cost-effective to revise the current control system to allow monitoring of all changes.'

If this tone sounds familiar, it should. One of the signatories of the report was Sir Robert Marshall, an Accounting Officer with a lot to account for.

The passage of Sir Robert over a decade reveals more than his own hapless destiny; it is symptomatic of the confusion and stresses in Whitehall as, one after another, the totems of True Brit were put into the hands of the Custodians. Sir Robert became under secretary at the Ministry of Aviation in 1964, just as that ministry was grappling with the appetite of Concorde. In 1966 he moved up a rung and into the Ministry of Power, where the North Sea oil contracts were administered, and where in 1968 he was awarded his C.B. In 1970 he became second permanent secretary at the Ministry of Technology in the last months of its life, where the Rolls Royce story was moving towards its denouement. The Ministry of Technology was swallowed by the Department of Trade and Industry, where Sir Robert got his K.C.B. and became, as the Secretary (Industry) one of the two top civil servants – and where all the chickens were coming home to roost, including the then rapacious Concorde. (Concorde had flown through the Ministry of Aviation, the Ministry of Technology, the Ministry of Aviation Supply, the D.T.I., and the Procurement Executive of the Ministry of Defence.) Late in 1973 Sir Robert moved from the D.T.I. to the Department of the Environment after failing to persuade Peter Walker to introduce petrol rationing.

All at sea with the Royal Navy:
The torpedo that disappeared and other excursions

In 1966 the Royal Navy wanted a new torpedo. It was supposed to be developed quickly and cheaply – at not more than £1m. In 1968 the Navy revised the design to get better performance 'at little expense'. In 1970 outside consultants were called in to examine the project, then called the Mark 31 torpedo. They reported that to complete it would cost £14m., and would take five-and-a-half years longer than had been predicted in 1966. By that time it would be obsolete.

The Mark 31 torpedo was then abandoned, having cost £5·25m. The Navy bought an American torpedo instead. The epitaph on the Mark 31 comes from Sir Michael Cary of the Ministry of Defence's Procurement Executive, in his evidence to the Public Accounts Committee:

> It is almost tragic in a way, reading the early files on this. The note of confidence which was struck, which was so falsified by later events, is rather sad. They were totally confident to start with that this was an easy, quick, cheap development totally within their capability. They emphasised that all the components had been tried in service and there were no unknowns. The only problem was that of compatibility. They were to have early trials to satisfy themselves that everything would be all right.
>
> In the light of what later happened when these incompatibilities gradually led to the total disappearance of the weapon, it is rather sad ...

Rule Britannia.

Sir Michael's tone of mournful understatement recurs in the accounts of other fiascos. With the equally droll Sir Robert Marshall he was called to explain the handling of the RB211 contract, and said: 'Monitoring is no substitute for management. We do not provide management.'

This was clear from several of the Navy's own misadventures. There was the case of the cruiser H.M.S. *Blake*. She was laid up in 1965 for a refit, planned to take eighteen months and to cost £5m. It took four years and cost £6·7 million. But that was not the end of the *Blake*'s troubles. Half-way through her post-refit trials True Brit intervened. In 1970 the Naval Staff decided to mark the bicentenary of Captain Cook's exploration of the Pacific by sending a battleship to the Far East 'to show the flag'. Unfortunately the supply of serviceable battleships was so depleted that the *Blake*, despite the fact that her trials were incomplete, had to be pressed into service. On the way to the Far East two of her boilers 'burned out', reducing her to an ignominious crawl, and the time she should have spent showing the flag was spent instead having expensive repairs in Singapore and Hong Kong.

The *Blake*'s sister cruiser, H.M.S. *Tiger*, was the victim of an even more expensive mistake. Assigned to a similar refit, again projected to cost £5m., the *Tiger* was stuck in the Devonport dockyard for five-and-a-half years. For long periods she was left 'opened up' and exposed to the elements, without any work being done. She literally began to rot away. The cost of putting this right, added to the planned work, came to £13·25m., which meant that refitting both ships had doubled in cost to £20m.

The Devonport dockyard is afflicted with more than derelict working methods. It has become a casualty of confusion in the upper ranks of the Custodians. In an effort to reform the dockyard's management an I.C.I. executive was drafted in to change the organization. This was the first cool eye from outside that Devonport had seen, and it looks like being the last. After eighteen months the I.C.I. man left and was replaced by a retired Rear-Admiral with a civil-service rank. Originally the dockyard was under Treasury control, but in the Whitehall reorganization it had fallen into the hands of the Civil Service Department. Miffed by their exclusion from the new Downing Street caucus, the Custodians of the C.S.D. became meddlesome lower down the line, which included taking over the day-to-day management of the Devonport dockyard.

The various arms of the Navy are fiercely jealous of their own projects, and some are stronger than others. Surface ships get more funds than submarines, and yet the submarines are virtually the only viable defence system the

Navy offers. Indulgences like the refits of the *Blake* and the *Tiger* are carried out at the expense of the submarines, and the guided-weapons programme, which included the Mark 31 torpedo, has ended up by at least doubling the cost of every missile it develops. In five years the development of the Seawolf missile went from £5m. to £10m., and even then it arrived too late to be fitted to the new cruisers and destroyers which are supposed to be dependent on it for defence against other missiles.

The Navy is still the most blimp-ridden of the services, top-heavy with gold braid and yet a pale shadow of the force it was in the days of empire. The naval staff seem to compensate by playing madcap games which have their denouement in fiscal and managerial catastrophes. For example, the ultimate object of the £20m. spent on the *Blake* and the *Tiger* was to put eight helicopters to sea on the cruisers. The alliance of the admirals, dreaming their gunboat fantasies, and the Custodians who provide the cash is, as Sir Michael Cary would say, 'rather sad'.

On the road with John Bullshit

It was such good news that the dealers bought space in the papers to announce it: the Ford cars being sold in Switzerland would no longer be shipped from Britain, but from Germany. The models made by Ford in Britain and Cologne are outwardly identical. But they do have one hidden difference: workmanship. The British Fords left a trail of dissatisfied customers in Switzerland. In the age of mass production the human touch is still detectable.

The same thing had happened in America. The Ford sports car, the Capri, is built in Britain and Germany, but the German output went to the U.S.A. because American dealers complained of British workmanship. Even Henry Ford himself, launching a new Mustang model in Detroit, took time off to moan in public about sloppy work in Britain. Ford had already brusquely told Edward Heath that Britain was too risky for dependable supply.

Plagued though it was, British Ford is, by the standards of the country, the most skilfully managed car plant in Britain, an uncomfortable token that Detroit training was best. British Leyland, that ailing hybrid of Lord Stokes's creation, turns out fewer than six vehicles a year per worker. Toyota turns out 59. And yet each flag-waving announcement by Stokes is greeted with the same frenzy that used to attend Nelson's victories at sea. The country *wants* to believe its own propaganda. But the British car manufacturers threw away the kind of chance that only comes once.

After World War II wiped out European car plants the British had the world market at their feet. Most countries were short of dollars, and Britain's colonial network gave her access to Africa, the Middle East and Asia as well as the non-captive markets in Europe. By 1950 Britain exported more cars than the U.S.A. But rather than design cars to suit foreigners, the British produced a bewildering variety of models created for the domestic snobbery of the 1930s, with fancy badges and shoddy performance. There was little after-sales back-up. Instead of winning markets, these lemons poisoned the well.

By 1956 Germany was able to overtake Britain as the top car-exporter, virtually on the reputation of the Beetle alone. Between 1964 and 1970 British car exports slumped from 21·7 per cent of the world market to 13·4 per cent. The Japanese followed the Germans in wiping up the world business and then joined them in cleaning up in the British home market, where both are now strongly established. Nearly a third of the cars sold in Britain are foreign-made. A half of the industry is American-owned. Becoming desperate under this pressure, Lord Stokes called for restrictions on imports, but it was too late.

British exports now depend largely on either luxury cars or sports cars. Neither is an idea created for foreign markets. Both happen to be British specialities which fill gaps left by conventional mass-production. And both depend more and more on mystique rather than a sense of value for money. The anxiety to own a piece of mobile True Brit is very forgiving. Take, for example, that different breed of cat, the Jaguar.

The Jaguar has always been as much a cult as a car. It has the aura of the thoroughbred. But there are really two Jaguars, the one in the mind, helped by the ad-man, and the one in the garage. In America the Jaguar is sold as a specialized 'road car', a tonic for the uncertain libido. The Jaguar is also regarded as a piece of hand-crafted machinery.

In truth, the Jaguar is a brilliantly designed car made in a crowded and over-strained plant. Both before and after it passed into the rag-bag of British Leyland the company has been so under-capitalized that it could never meet demand. This pressure to turn out more cars in spite of the plant has dimmed the passions of many a buck as, *en route* to some idyllic assignation, an expensive noise erupts from somewhere in the machinery.

In Britain, Jaguar's image has moved away from the passion wagon to satisfying the more bourgeois urges of the business executive who wants the comforts of a saloon with a tinge of the sports car, rather like a wistfully flickering memory of pleasures past and fruits long since picked. The XJ6 saloon caught this demand so perfectly that the company's previous underestimates of demand seem in comparison to be minor. The plant could crank out only 120 XJ6s a week (when it was not strike-bound), creating such a scarcity value that a black market developed. A second-hand XJ6 sold for £5,250 – £1,500 over the list price. Many customers thought the car was *underpriced* – in other words, not exclusive enough. Jaguar exploited this snobbery in an ad: 'We're doing all we can to stop the car falling into the wrong hands, so that people like you can enjoy the ecstasy without the agony of waiting too long or paying more than you should.' The waiting list ran anything up to two years, a long while for those sublimated satyrs who make the Jaguar such a hot property.

Buy me, I'm the real True Brit

Lured into humiliation by the Impossible Dream, and leaving a trail of lemons on the roads of the world, True Brit is left in the market place secure only with a sentimental kind of appeal, distilled – if that is not too much of a pun – in the world of the whisky ads. Whisky is so near to being a God-given essence (try Japanese whisky and see how divine that is) that it would take real genius to spoil it. But the glass of whisky has been portrayed by the advertising agency photographers as something which wraps up a way of life – drink the stuff and you turn into True Brit ...

The man is probably in his country tweeds. He has a way of leaning on the palings of the horse farm so that the creases all fall right. He'll have on his flat tweed cap; the important thing about the cap is the way his hair falls out from under it. Generations of barbering have gone into the cut of that hair. True Brit has always worn his hair just a little bit long at the back. They cut it like that at Eton, although True Brit probably never went to Eton. There used to be something slightly, well – slightly effeminate about that hair, flopping over the collar at the back. But not any more.

In his selling mode, True Brit has companions, three of them. A horse, a dog, and a woman, in that order. The horse is a thoroughbred, probably stud. The woman has also been carefully bred, just like the horse, to be dumb but elegant. She has one of those long white necks, one string of pearls. One for class, two for flash, three for bad taste. Only women in the Royal Family who don't know any better wear three strings of pearls. She also wears Sensible Shoes. Sensible Shoes are more than shoes, they are a state of mind. The impress of *control*. Sensible Shoes know how far to go, and they will never go further. At least, not in a whisky ad.

The dog is probably an Irish setter. Dogs and horses are two of the things the Irish do well. True Brit is very careful about the Irish: he won't touch their whiskey (which is why he insists that they put the 'e' in it, to ensure segregation) and he'll seldom touch their women. But the dogs and the horses, they can be made to behave.

In this role True Brit is truly himself. He is not over-reaching, he is not out of character, he can handle it. Whether it's whisky, pottery, fake antiques, men's clothes, Sensible Shoes, sporting guns – all the accoutrements of his decadent tastes – then you can trust him. He knows those games, they are a part of his breeding, the stamp of his class. But if he appears as the new *wunderkind* of technology, keep your distance. He's not himself.

18 *Sex Goes Public :*
Learning to live with the Rampant Penis

'*At first she hit Miss G with a plastic belt. Then Mr Z and Miss G tied her to the bed and after Miss G had left Mr Z hit her with his hand on her bottom.*' – MISS L, witness in a London court

What's going on here? Somebody is having some fun; somebody has been caught having some fun; somebody is being made to suffer for having that fun (though not by the use of a plastic belt); some people are going to get away with it, since they have been granted alphabetical anonymity. Here are the basic ingredients of the British way of sex: flagellation, bondage, arse-worship and institutional reprisal.

There is no statistical proof that the British are more sexually resourceful than the Germans, French or Japanese. There is evidence that the British public-school system encourages buggery, but not that it invented it. The French may believe, as they apparently do, that flagellation is *une vice anglaise*. But this may be nothing better than a cherished stereotype. The British have, in any case, come to suspect that the French libido is an exaggeration. After decades of believing in naughty Paris, the British now regard it as a Puritan backwater.

The curiosity of the British way of sex lies not in its technical quality, but in the social and political attitudes attached to it. The same flame licks the loins of the British as of anyone else, but somewhere between the erogenous zones and the head funny things start to happen.

Sex has not been a recent discovery in Britain, it has just

gone public. It takes a lot of getting used to. The libertine life was once much more of a private activity. Privacy is very much a privilege; you have to be able to afford it. This meant that the rich and the powerful were the best concealed when they played games. And this created the misleading impression that they didn't play, at least not much.

The idea of sexual equality is as disturbing to the British ruling caste as the ideas of equality of wealth or opportunity. Moral superiority is an indispensable part of authority; if it goes it becomes impossible for the powerful to impose moral sanctions on others. The more that the rulers are caught with their pants down in public; the more exposed is their cant. It is the worst kind of indignity, and as they are being caught more often they become both ludicrous and more vengeful. Their fury is increased because, in going public, sex has been avidly taken up by the people. All over London you can see the smile of knowingness. Sex in Britain has become *accessible* – which means more than available. The first requirement of accessibility is knowledge; if you know how to do it, why it is done, then you can expect to enjoy it. Enjoying it, the Victorian sin, is much easier now. And that is precisely what makes the Puritans mad.

The Puritan backlash – it might almost be another sexual innovation – has surfaced under strange leadership, the union of an ex-schoolmistress and an eccentric Anglo–Irish peer. The result is a kind of moral Powellism.

It took Mrs Mary Whitehouse about nine years to progress from a nobody to a busybody. In her blue-rinsed hair, winged glasses and Sensible Shoes, Mrs Whitehouse represents the kind of modesty that becomes tyrannical because of its persistence. She is the incarnation of the British matriarchy, driven by some menopausal paranoia into believing that lost virginity will bring down the nation. Sexual ignorance was upheld by the Victorians by calling it 'mystery', something dark between the sheets forever mute. Mrs Whitehouse subscribes to the Mystery of Sex.

Her own parents thought it so private a subject that they never discussed it with her in any explicit way – a situation that for all the progress since made is probably still fairly common. 'You must be careful,' they said to her, enigmatically. They relied on their daughter's capacity for self-instruction: 'Growing up as I did in the 'twenties, as part of a generation which found no difficulty in talking about sex – though by no means obsessed by it – I gradually accumulated understanding and, I hope, responsibility. By the time I was grown up the sense of "naughtiness" had gone but not, I'm happy to say, the mystery.'

One reason why Mary Whitehouse has become a formidable leader of the Morality Police is that she looks so believable and so ordinary, an anti-intellectual when so many of the libertines come across as a patronizing and depraved intelligentsia. Another reason is that she has picked her targets shrewdly.

Her earliest and major successes were at the expense of the B.B.C. Over the years she has portrayed the B.B.C. television service as an intruding philanderer, corrupting the innocent with its worldly humours, its lascivious dramas and its impertinent treatment of authority. At first the B.B.C. made the fatal error of ignoring her. But inch by inch, through subtle psychological propaganda, she unnerved the B.B.C. leadership and wrung humiliating concessions from them.

The B.B.C. became so unravelled that it proclaimed a new programme code to placate its critics. In the course of this it apologized for a scene in the acclaimed historical series 'Elizabeth R' in which a naked girl was seen 'leaving the bed of the King of France'. The author of the episode responded brusquely that the girl had been in bed with the Duke of Alençon, 'not the King of France, who would have been more likely to have been in bed with a small boy'. If the B.B.C. can't tell the difference between a satyr and a pederast it is really in trouble.

For Frank, Lord Longford, the point on the road to the

sexual Damascus was a performance of 'Oh! Calcutta!' He
walked out half-way through: 'It was only intended to
shock with sexual display ... when I realised that it couldn't
be prosecuted, I suddenly felt we were in danger of seeing
all the defences against obscenity washed away.' This reaction set Longford on a course which has earned him the
dubious crown of Anti-Pornographer Royal (with Kenneth
Tynan as the Pornographer Royal). Like Mrs Whitehouse,
Longford converts private phantoms into public threats.
After his conversion, he went straight to the hardest of hard
cores, Denmark.

Denmark now plays a part in the British libido that was
once, in grander days, filled by Port Said. The gymnastic
Arab pornography, with its predilection for sodomy, has
given way in popularity to nubile Nordic inventions.
Danish hard-core comes under plain covers into numerous
British suburban bowers, and Danish swiving manuals,
books, magazines, and movies pour into the warehouses of
British pornographers.

Longford went to study the phenomenon first hand, as it
were, only to be embarrassed on his return when the
Customs opened his bags and found them bulging with
fruity literature. He explained that it was all research
material for a massive study on pornography, for which he
had recruited a committee of fifty. Longford is a bizarre
figure: the high, bald dome like Queen Elizabeth's death-
mask, rather dishevelled appearance, nervous, jerky man-
nerism, and fluty, lispish upper-class voice. Old Etonian,
once a Tory and then a Socialist, once a Protestant then a
Catholic, a don, an Irish patriot, banker, publisher, and
inveterate do-gooder, he is engagingly self-mocking and
eminently mockable. His anti-sexual crusade is his most
visible act, and out of key with a private penchant for spicy
gossip.

When the Longford Report appeared it looked more like
a pulp novel, with the word 'Pornography' in $2\frac{1}{4}$-inch red
capitals on the cover. At the press conference launching it

Longford and Mary Whitehouse ran into Xaviera Hollander, the Happy Hooker, cashing-in on the occasion to push her own memoirs. Carnality met chastity and smiled decorously at each other. The report enjoyed a massive but brief attention, then rightly faded away. A few weeks later, when *Last Tango in Paris* opened in London, Longford was one of the first in line for tickets. 'If you criticize pornography as I have done you should be prepared to see what you criticize', he explained. Certainly nobody can claim that he is derelict in that.

> Mr Justice Phillimore was trying a sodomy case and brooded greatly whether his judgment had been right. He went to consult Birkenhead. 'Excuse me, My Lord, but could you tell me – what do you think one ought to give a man who allows himself to be buggered?' 'Oh, thirty shillings or two pounds, anything you happen to have on you.' – 1920s Oxford joke

Longford was at Oxford while that joke was current. So were many of the Custodians who now glower down from the benches of the law on the sexual carnival, their loins as dry as their wit. It is not so easy now for them to retain the composure of moral impeccability. Their cover has been blown. There was a diarist in their midst; the kind of man who didn't obey the code, a middle-class snob ingratiating himself into the elite to record their depravities. His name was Evelyn Waugh.

What Scott Fitzgerald did for the Flappers, Waugh did simultaneously for the orgiastic British upper classes. *Vile Bodies* and *Decline and Fall* were taken as satire and, in a way, not taken too seriously. You can always laugh at decadence so long as it is fictional. And as long as Waugh's world remained hermetically sealed in his lapidary prose the cover remained secure. But forty years later, exposed by his diaries, the Oxford and Mayfair of the 1920s putrefied as readily as a mummy with its bandages ripped off. The truth was more bizarre than the 'satire', and enough of the participants are still at large to require, for the sake of British libel laws, their names to be replaced by asterisks.

The diarist's revelations were so instantly embarrassing that a group of Waugh's Oxford contemporaries, showing all the signs of the attrition of unstinted sensuality, convened to explain them away. They took the elitist line. So much, they said, for the idea that permissiveness was invented in the 1960s. It was there all along. But only for those who were refined enough to appreciate it. Like a good vintage champagne, sex was too good for vulgar and untrained appetites. And with this characteristic conceit, they slumped into post-prandial comas, no doubt re-living the reverie of lost youth. But Waugh performed a posthumous service – he had caught the Custodians with their pants down.

'Last time I voted for the Tories, because they are my best clients,' said Mrs Norma Levy, sometime bedmate of Lord Lambton and others. In a government sombre with the work ethic, the Lords Lambton and Jellicoe were rare buds of life. After being caught philandering, both had to be sacrificed to the hypocrisy of the Morality Police. True, the engaging Tony Lambton once unwisely played moralist himself. In 1963 he wrote: 'One cannot doubt that the harm this will do the Conservative Party will be enormous', so putting the knife in for the fallen Minister of War, John Profumo, whose private tastes Lambton shared. Ten years later, caught by the 'image-intensive' infra-red camera of the *News of the World* in the *ménage à trois* of Mrs Levy, and smoking pot, Lambton could ruefully reflect: 'One of the frailties of human nature is that one can very often see things in other people which one cannot see in oneself.'

One puzzle of this affair was: were the aristos the last ones left in London who didn't know that it was free? Or was there some perverse kick in paying for it, even when you knew your record in seduction was dandy? Lambton's answer was disarming: 'People sometimes like variety.' And people sometimes like slumming.

But his answer was more convincing than the appallingly

self-righteous tone of the House of Commons when Lambton and Jellicoe were expelled from that club. It took the form of the spinsterish meanness, the reprisal of the men who dare not on those who dare, which the British like to indulge. And the episode provoked a typical essay in kneejerk moralism by *The Times*. 'The Protestant ethic', wrote the Catholic editor of *The Times*, 'is not crumbling by sectors, it is the whole line of cliffs that is being eroded by the sea ... the traditional standards of British public life are under attack.' But the traditional standards of British public life include graft, corruption, bribes, lies, exploitation, persecution, and perversions.

Nobody epitomizes the myth of Victorian rectitude more than Gladstone. Although he never strayed sexually, Victoria's eccentric Prime Minister had a curious taste for the company of prostitutes, hoping to be able to redeem them with rhetoric. Gladstone knew well enough that British politics spoke with two voices, those of the public platform and the private pillow. He once said he had known eleven other Prime Ministers and seven were adulterers. Two, the Duke of Wellington and Lord Palmerston, were among the regular clients of the brothel run by Harriette Wilson and her sisters Fanny and Amy.

Lloyd George was the last really randy Prime Minister. He had the morals of one of his native Welsh mountain goats. 'Love is all right, if you lose no time', he said. He lost little time, and no opportunity. After him, British governments passed into the custody of men who were apparently too busy with affairs of state to try anything on the side. But the traditional cover of discretion protected the spicy lives of many of their juniors.

Lambton and Jellicoe were martyred for the pretence of a tradition that was fraudulent; like Profumo they had to go because they were caught. Lords of the realm must not let the side down – but they can be let off lightly: Norma Levy, on trivial charges, was bailed only on the enormous sum of £10,000, another sign of the Stephen Ward scapegoat syn-

drome. It is not the British bedroom that is threatened by
the Rampant Penis, but the British system.

The greatest sensitivity to sexual freedom is political, not
moral. The salacious passages in Waugh's diaries were embarrassing because of the identity of the participants, not the
nature of the activity. Breaches of what was once a private
depravity well-concealed behind the lives of public figures
threaten the right of a charmed circle to continue its rule.

There are attempts to write off these revelations as peculiar to the Bohemian Bloomsbury set. Nigel Nicolson's
revelatory 'Portrait of a Marriage', containing the amours of
his sapphist mother and predatory homosexual father, has
extended the picture of Bloomsbury's ambisextrous confusion. But this was no isolated pocket of upper-class life,
merely the least discreet and most voluble. And it was as
hypocritical as the rest. Writers who piously censured Victorian humbug were themselves dependent on social double-
standards. The British are not cock-shy. They are truth-shy.

19 The Final Legacy of True Brit:
'Over the hills and a great way off ... '

'Keep then the sea, the wall of our England, And then is England kept by God's own hand' – The Libel of English Policy, 1436

Islanders are different. There is always something parlous about living on an island. In Britain the elements seem to be in a fine balance: a sympathetic land, a sly sea. And the British are, before anything else, islanders. It is not just a state of mind but a condition. Boring a hole under the English Channel will not change it. It cannot move the country thirty miles further to the east.

Being an islander is not necessarily bad. It makes a nation finite in a way that lines drawn on maps have notoriously failed to do. It helps to give credence to the otherwise dubious notion of national separateness. Feeling British induces a precise definition of what is alien: it is anything across the water.

The trouble is that while the British are insular in their minds they are worldly in their needs. The country's dependence on forces beyond its control has steadily increased. The British are caught in the volatile tides of international trade and money without having their old primacy in either. This vulnerability has not wholly sunk in; True Brit cannot concede it. Over the last few decades the uncertainty of supply of those things which support life on the island has coincided with a hardening of the conviction that the condition of being an island is 'kept by God's own hand'. Not only must this not be compromised, it must be reinforced.

In such a state of mind the appeal of journeys back in the Time Machine is obvious. The preferred 'greatness' lies backwards, somewhere in that time-zone where the myths and heroes are. Ahead lies only uncertainty and an unnerving contest.

By an odd irony, what the British perceive as their own qualities are also looked at longingly by others, although not because they have anything to do with survival in a competitive world. A survey of European businessmen conducted at Sussex University revealed that, given a choice of birthplace, more would choose to be born British than anything else. The Belgians, the Dutch, and the Italians also favoured the idea of their boss being British. On the other hand the Germans were regarded as the most competent in any job. Congeniality is not, alas, enough.

Foreigners are apt to make generalizations about the British character, such as: 'The British are lazy'. But what appears to be laziness is a weariness and fatalism about the uselessness of effort when the rewards are so minimal. The recurrent exhortations to work harder in the cause of True Brit have done little to alter the country's traditional biases. The British can be as hard-driving as anybody when the rewards are plentiful, as they are for the property developer and the asset-stripper.

The real beneficiaries of the British value-system are still mostly those who make the least contribution to society. Saying this appears to repeat the doctrine of the far left; but what distinguishes the British condition from a theoretical model of the capitalist system is the powerful hold of True Brit on both the defenders of the system and those who are supposed to be its opponents. The apparent conflicts of the two major political parties are basically false, because the policies of both dare not (even if they wanted to) move away from those mythical moorings of 'national greatness'. There is a feeling of some awful, barely restrained spectre which, simply by being glimpsed, will destroy the national will. The name of this spectre is truth. It is not the kind of truth that comes to a nation after a period of sustained lying and deception, as it has to America after the Watergate affair. Those are the corruptions of individual power-seeking. The truth that the British are thought to be unready to face is a universal and ultimately inevitable one: that they cannot be what they were. It is not such a dreadful thing to have to face. But just try to say it.

The most unexpected apostle of the Awful Truth turned up in the form of Lord Rothschild. What he said in a speech at Wantage in September 1973 was neither new nor – since it came from Lord Rothschild – uncouthly expressed. 'There must be a major national change of orientation,' he said. 'We have to think twice about the desirability of courses of action which, in the distant past, were ours by right. We have to realize that we have neither the money nor the resources to do all those things we should like to do and so often we feel we have the right to do.' Then, to rub home his point, Rothschild echoed Hermann Kahn's prediction that by 1985 Britain would be the poorest nation in Europe. What Lord Rothschild got for his trouble was an immediate reprimand from his boss, Edward Heath, and an orgy of hysterical True Brit from the newspapers, one of which called him 'Lord Doom'. As a civil servant, albeit temporary, Rothschild was supposed to keep his mouth shut and his head down. But sitting as he was at the heart of that bunker in Whitehall where the Custodians pursue their fantasies, Rothschild had seen too much and thought it was about time to blow the whistle. All he succeeded in doing was to demonstrate the impossibility of reversing the slide. Given its myopic state, Britain's ultimate standing seems likely to be alongside other husks of empire like Spain and Portugal.

Rothschild's suggested remedy was to recapture 'the mentality we had during World War II'. What he failed to see was that the 'blitz spirit' was induced by a common and alien threat: the persistent sickness of the country in peacetime is the inevitable result of a society not threatened so much from outside as riven from inside by the cancer of class, and the inequities which remain entrenched.

There has been exactly a decade in which this decline might have been faced up to and perhaps reversed. The Rubicon of the new British politics came in 1964. This was when the country had to face the crunch of lost primacy. If it had been like other European societies, it would have been pulled towards the American ideal of a middle-class consensus with only marginal ideological distinctions. For the Labour party, as the more doctrinaire of the two, this meant paying lip-service to its old ideals while trying at the same time to seem capable of the managerial skills to overhaul industry. National survival was more pressing than social engineering. In that way Wilson became committed to the corporate state. He created the unprecedented axis of capitalism and the government machine. But he was also as susceptible to the delusions of True Brit as a die-hard imperialist. And it is now clear, from the confessions of people like Barbara Castle, Richard Crossman, and Wilson's own personal secretary, that the Labour ministers were inadequately prepared for power and that their ideals were easily subverted by the Custodians who ran them. In theory they ought to have been more likely to recognize the fatal social flaw that Kahn alighted on – 'with slow growth like yours the rich get richer and the poor get poorer' – and to have dismantled the old, static wealth. Instead they were diverted from social priorities by the pressures of a recurrent economic malaise without realizing that that malaise had a social origin. The rich did get richer, and more of the poor got poorer.

But the political failure is not, at root, one of social or economic theory. These are, after all, only tools. In themselves they do not induce sanity. What has rendered a decade of promises nugatory is True Brit. Through six of those years Harold Wilson wandered, looking more and more like Beatrix Potter's Pigling Bland ('Over the hills and a great way off, the wind shall blow my top knot off'). At the beginning was his promise of a wind of change, at the end only wind. Later, moving with all the consistency of a weathercock, he renounced the trespasses of the technocratic machine which he had himself authored and promised instead of a kind of populism. For his own self-survival he had to revert to the old Socialist dogma, to forget 1964 and recall 1945. The trouble is that Socialism breeds big government and big business. Wilson's left wing, under the propulsion of Anthony Wedgwood Benn, technical *apparatchik*, now sees its utopia in the nationalization of the twenty-five largest industrial companies, a prospect of bureaucratic paralysis surpassing even the Heathian horrors.

Nothing puts a British politician's social intentions more on the line than educational policy. The school system directly supports the class system; if you want to dismantle one you have to dismantle the other. This is why educational reform alarms the middle class more than anything else. Muddled experiments with new schools in the name of social equality have created a surge in demand for the safe and unchanging priorities of the education that only money can buy. There are 227,000 children at independent schools, 107,000 as boarders. Soaring fees are no deterrent. It now costs £1,000 a year to send a boy to Winchester (Eton and Harrow are a shade cheaper). Since there are supposed to be only about 100,000 people in Britain earning £10,000 a year or more, the ability of many to pay these fees is something of a mystery.

The self-perpetuating dedication of the British elite is impressive. The prospect of a truly levelled society is too wretched for them to contemplate. As well as buying a better education, the middle class can purchase private medical treatment and by-pass any of the other inconveniences of the Welfare State. They have the savvy to work the system. They did not invent the impediment of lowly birth, but they are damned sure that they are not going to do anything to remove it.

Class is not the guide to party allegiances that it once was.

Wilson's victory in 1964 depended on a defection by a considerable number of middle-class Tories. Until then 85 per cent of Labour's support was working class. In 1966 Wilson increased his middle-class appeal; by 1970 he had lost it, and the election. But it is now not only the middle-class vote that strays. The working-class vote in many areas follows a racist impulse and goes wherever the most hawkish noises are made about immigration. It is a volatile and unpredictable situation in which the inchoate and opportunist Liberal party now gains at the expense of the other two. But if ever a party looked unready for power it is the Liberals.

In fact, as the receptacle of the disenchanted, all the Liberals have to do is to be there with open arms. And as the party with a traditional appeal to property-owners, there was a growing supply of recruits. The dream of the 1960s, held out by Harold Macmillan, was of 'a property-owning democracy'. The dream has been fulfilled to a striking extent. At the beginning of the century only 10 per cent of the British owned their own homes. In the last generation the proportion has gone from a quarter to over a half. Many of these new home-owners are working-class.

This ought to have profound social implications. Nothing increases the conservative instinct more than the ownership of property, which leads to a whole clutch of other expectations. But the property-owning dream has turned out, for the working class, to be a trap. They had none of the resources of inherited wealth, personal savings, or the middle-class ability to deal with banks and lawyers. With the onset of chronic inflation, soaring interest rates and frozen wages, they have been screwed. They cannot fall back into their old working-class culture, and they are equally distant from the class above. If any single group brings down the new politics it will be the impoverished property-owners.

In this kind of mood it would be easy for the British to turn to atavism. Encouraged by Enoch Powell, they sense that somewhere beyond the contemporary plagues is that Valhalla of empire where a simpler and non-competitive life can be rediscovered, a kind of pastoral version of True Brit. An opt-out seems appealing, because it would leave the driving and thrusting to the Germans, French, Japanese, and anybody else interested in the fast buck. Political exhortations to become more pushy, more greedy and more nasty like everybody else don't get a sympathetic hearing. That wetness which Edward Heath so abhors is seeping in.

Heath himself offers the classic example of the man isolated by power to the point where whatever instincts he once had for the public mood have long since dried into a peevish frustration. Desperate to inspire, but unable to communicate, he lapsed into tantrums. Marooned one night at the House of Commons by a traffic jam, he had to walk the few hundred yards back to Downing Street. By the time he got there he was so angry that he ordered a complaint about the traffic to be telephoned to the head of the Greater London Council. As it happened, this scapegoat was in Tokyo, at a conference on urban blight. But the call was put through to him just the same. It was, of course, the kind of inconvenience that ordinary people in London have to suffer every day. But Heath had developed the sensitivity of a monarch.

The Heath administration came to represent more than a new kind of managerial Conservatism; it was the apotheosis of all the fantasies which both parties had pursued during the 'sixties and early 'seventies, the most philistine phase of True Brit. The men who prospered during this time, commercially and politically, were of a kind. Nobody represents this breed more than Peter Walker, who bridged business and politics in a deliberate and – according to the values of the day – inevitable rise to one of the most powerful positions in the land. Walker is a pedestrian speaker and, as his propaganda for the 'New Capitalism' showed, a banal philosopher. But to Heath he offered that simplistic ruthlessness which was imagined to be the required laxative for a constipated economy.

Heath's government evolved further from Cabinet control than any other, and bore a striking resemblance to the clandestine corporate structure of a multi-national corporation like I.T.T. There was Heath, the obsessive chief executive; there was his favoured 'inner Cabinet'; and there were the Custodians as the submerged and omnipotent operational arm, arguably the most lastingly powerful group in the country. The 'inner Cabinet', in effect the executive committee of Great Britain Ltd, had to operate through the anonymous Cabinet committees where the Custodians deployed the myth of their own expertise, and set the limits on policy.

Heath's acolytes in the 'inner Cabinet' reflect his own tastes and priorities; as well as Walker there was Anthony Barber, a tax lawyer and financial director; Robert Carr, metallurgical engineer, and an ex-director of several companies including Securicor; Jim Prior, ex-chairman of a company which built boats and agricultural machinery: all self-made businessmen who had risen outside the orthodox channels of the League of Gentlemen. Government in Britain is a frustrating experience for a self-made man; the zealots around Edward Heath soon began to show that impatience of men confronted by a system which is not easily dislodged. It had broken Wilson, and his ideologues.

The aptitudes of a Labour Cabinet are those of the middle-class academic and professional man; business managers are rare among them. Wilson's policies required managers, and they had to come either from outside or – as a masquerade – from the Custodians. Although Heath had groomed his Hustlers for power, they were no better able than their ideological opposites to wrest control either from its traditional base in the City, or from the Custodians. Instead, they too fell in with the manner of True Brit. Selsdon Man, that 1970 dose of salts, has long since gone.

Heath's unlovely insouciance springs from the temper of a covetous bureaucrat. Twenty years earlier, as a civil servant, he was one of the planners of London Airport – Heathrow. His modern megatheria, expressing itself in an even bigger airport, motorways, tunnels, and other flights of technological heroism, became all-consuming. Like Wilson before him, Heath's fantasies were maintained at the expense of social remedy. Once infected by it, the victim finds that True Brit is irreversible.

In the truest sense, Britain is a deeply corrupted country. Effective power has been taken from its rightful place and consolidated in the hands of people with the means to use it and at the same time to remain anonymous. But there has been no sudden and complete conspiracy. Power has been allowed to move in this way because of preference and convenience rather than by intrigue. True Brit has been the lubricant of this process. The motive of the power elite is essentially preservationist – the retention of the *status quo*. Their own guarantee of permanence is in the respectability of upholding the values of True Brit.

Very few political decisions today can be intuitive. Life is too complex for that. With Parliament still obsessed by its belief in the purity of the amateur and the spell of gab, it is open to anybody claiming 'expertise' to baffle the people with science. But in Britain 'expertise' has become as much a mystique as gab. The Custodians appropriated their now swollen powers by the pretence of expertise, and although their record is risible they have no challengers because they have no accountability. The catastrophe of their regime has been, by their own arranging, largely invisible. And invisibility requires two things: a talent for concealment and a consenting blindness in those who ought to be watching.

A Note on Sources

Where it seemed important to the point being made, references for material used have been quoted in the text itself. However, it would have been tedious to list chapter and verse for every statistic. For the benefit of readers who may want to follow up certain points, a short list of sources is given below. The place of publication is London unless otherwise stated.

The author has drawn on many other sources. The cataract of public documents published by H.M. Stationery Office (at the expense of a continuing deficit) is for some reason largely ignored in the Press. It is eccentric in its range and variable in its quality but deserves attention from all students of the British condition; buried within it are facts and episodes that intimidate invention.

The author is also grateful to the staff of the London Library for providing the resources and ambience which remove much of the pain from research.

Government and the Civil Service

New Trends in Government by Sir Richard Clarke (H.M.S.O., 1971). An unusually revealing analysis by a former senior Treasury mandarin, the text of six lectures given to the Civil Service Staff College and, one hopes, not doomed to fall on deaf ears.
The British Political Elite by W. L. Guttsman (MacGibbon and Kee, 1963) – a dispassionate diagnosis of the workings of the magic circle and its historical roots.
Elites and Their Education by David Boyd (National Foundation for Educational Research, 1973) – the most current research on self-perpetuation via public schools and Oxbridge.

Policy Making in Britain edited by Richard Rose (Macmillan Student Editions, 1969) – useful study of the innermost bureacracies in action.

Case histories

Official reports are disabled by both the limitations on Parliamentary scrutiny and the censorship of evidence before publication. But some hair-raising stuff does slip through.

Committee of Public Accounts, *First Report, 1972–73* (H.M.S.O.) – the tenacious and knowledgeable Harold Lever stalks the Custodians as they answer for the North Sea Oil fiasco; some of it reads like a novel, though the net result is ineffably sad.

Committee of Public Accounts, *Third Report, 1971–72* (H.M.S.O.) – a catalogue of maladministration, including the denouement of Rolls Royce.

The Expenditure Committee, *Ninth Report, 1971–72* (H.M.S.O.). This puny body is supposed to function as an early warning system, rather than the pool of hindsight which the Public Accounts Committee provides; this report shows the hopelessness of the effort.

Select Committee on the Civil List, 1971–72, *Report* (H.M.S.O.) – the Queen's flunkeys submit their claims for more money, and Willie Hamilton blasts away, but surprisingly it is Roy Jenkins who makes the most pertinent republican-like noises.

Basic background

The British Constitution, a survey for students, by R. K. Mosley (Itchen Printers, Southampton): this little pamphlet, published annually, keeps track of quirks and misdemeanours and offers a useful bibliography.

The English Constitution by Walter Bagehot, introduction by Richard Crossman (Fontana, 1963) – despite Bagehot's obsolescent and euphoric interpretation, Crossman's ver-

sion is well worth study, though it pre-dates his own dis-
illusioning experiences in the Wilson government.

Incidental illumination

Philby by Bruce Page, David Leitch and Phillip Knightley
(Deutsch, 1968) – incomplete but devastating exposure of
elitism's soft underbelly.
Turn Again, Westminster by Woodrow Wyatt (Deutsch,
1973) – the diary of a love-hate relationship with the mother
of Parliaments, indicating its impotence and seductive
powers.
Freedom and Reality by Enoch Powell (Batsford, 1969) –
the paradoxical creed of the Last Englishman.
The Rise of Enoch Powell by Paul Foot (Cornmarket, 1969) –
useful historical analysis of Powell texts.
The State of the Nation: Parliament (Granada Publishing,
1973) – the transcripts of three ambitious television programmes in which senior Custodians and M.P.s reveal the
mess that they're both in. These scripts have been drawn on
for several quotations in Chapter 6.
'Factionalism within the Conservative Party: the Monday
Club' by Patrick Seyd, *Government and Opposition*, Vol. 7
No. 4, 1972 – objective and basic research on the ultra-
right.

The way we live now

Social Trends, Central Statistical Office (H.M.S.O., annual)
– invaluable and surprisingly comprehensive social statistics on everything from the law to polluted rivers.
The General Household Survey, Introductory Report
(H.M.S.O., 1973): the first mammoth bite into a new kind
of social survey, technical and dense but very telling.
'Class in Britain', *The Sociological Review*, Vol. 20, No. 3,
August 1972 – appallingly written in academic jargon, but
between the lines emerges a picture of the fraud of 'class-
lessness'.
Britain 2001 A.D. by Colin Leicester (H.M.S.O., 1972) –

a distinctly non-science-fiction vision of an over-consuming society.

One for Sorrow, Two for Joy edited by Paul Barker (Allen and Unwin, 1972) – anthology of ten years' output from the magazine *New Society*, ten years of national identity crisis recalled with perception.

'How the Poorest Live', *New Society*, 1973 – pamphlet reprinting a series of articles which blow the mask off the idea of the affluent society.

Money and Wealth

Some fundamental information about who is worth what is still missing, obligingly obscured by inadequate records. Best available sources are:

Institute of Statistics, Oxford, *Bulletin*, May 1961: pioneer work, though by self-admission fallible. Over the 1940s and 1950s disparities in personal wealth lessened, but this research pre-dates the land, property and business speculation fortunes.

Unequal Shares by A. B. Atkinson (Allen Lane, 1972) – more comprehensive and up-to-date, and much more alarming. Confirms the most lop-sided distribution of wealth in any western democracy.

National Income and Expenditure, Central Statistical Office (H.M.S.O., annual) – chronic balance sheet of Great Britain Ltd.

Environment

The Property Boom by Oliver Marriott (Pan, 1967) – first piece of whistle-blowing on rampant speculation.

The Recurrent Crisis of London (Counter Information Services, 1972) – who made what in the bonanza.

Goodbye London by Christopher Booker and Candida Lycett Green (Fontana, 1973) – detailed catalogue of priceless architecture mindlessly removed for profit.

Polluting Britain by Jeremy Bugler (Pelican, 1972) – shows how feeble are the safeguards against filth.

How to Play the Environment Game by Theo Crosby (Penguin Special, 1973) – how planning destroys people. Royal Commission on Environmental Pollution, *Third Report* (H.M.S.O., 1972) – and then they poisoned the sea.

Secrecy and Censorship

The Trial of Lady Chatterley by C. H. Rolph (Penguin, 1961) – now nostalgic watershed of literary licence.
Not in the Public Interest by David Williams (Hutchinson, 1965) – the Official Secrets Act and other malignancies subjected to learned scrutiny.
Censorship in Britain by Paul O'Higgins (Nelson, 1972) – a barrister's civilized attack on the secret society.
Against Censorship (National Council for Civil Liberties, 1972) – pamphlet bound to inflame Lord Chancellors.

Race Relations

Racial Discrimination in England by W. W. Daniel (Pelican, 1968) – first solid research on home-grown bigotry.
Police Power and Black People by Derek Humphry (Panther, 1972) – documentary evidence of floundering and sometimes brutal police response to immigrant problem.
Brothers to All Men? by Monty Meth (Runnymede Trust, 1972) – blatant discrimination by trade unions.
Select Committee on Race Relations, 1971–72, *Police/Immigrant Relations* (H.M.S.O.) – among other things the evidence destroys the myth of crime-prone coloured communities.
Black Britain by Chris Mullard (Allen and Unwin, 1973) – controlled and chilling memoir by a British-born black social worker, disillusioned by liberal paternalists.
Black Men, White Cities by Ira Katznelson (Oxford University Press, 1973) – scholarly comparison of the American and British race-relations industries, with the daunting conclusion that nothing has been learned by Britain from the American experience.

Education and class

Education and the Working Class by Brian Jackson and Dennis Marsden, Pelican, 1962 – case studies in Huddersfield of the social warp in schools.
'Transition from School to Work' by D. N. Ashton, *The Sociological Review*, Vol. 21, No. 1, February 1973 – how class pre-ordains performance even in comprehensives.

Business

Britain on Borrowed Time by Glyn Jones and Michael Barnes (Pelican, 1967) – from the shop floor to the boardroom, anachronism and inertia.
Business in Britain by Graham Turner (Pelican, 1969) – a rather adoring view of the business ethic but significant detail on the nexus of Whitehall and industry.
Thalidomide and the Power of the Drug Companies by Henning Sjostrom and Robert Nilsson (Penguin, 1972) – Swedish record of the international scandal.

Cops and robbers

Society and the Policeman's Role by Maureen E. Cain (Routledge and Kegan Paul, 1973) – objective sociological field-notes containing revealing evidence of the internal caste system and rituals of the police.
Inside the Underworld by Peta Fordham (Allen and Unwin, 1972) – by one of the few people who understands what British crooks are like, and how they are changing.

ib